for my girls

Savannah Ugan

Edited by Lauren Steffes

Details in some anecdotes have been changed to protect the identities of the persons involved.

ISBN: 9798653257094

Dedication

To my girls: Hannah H., Hannah S., Savannah, Caroline, Shannon, Mary Nell, Abigail, Emily, Kate, Katie, Jenn, Ashley, Liz, Ansley, Jamie, Tori, Lauren, Phebe, Parker, Lindsey, Gaby, Alafia, India, and Haley. Thank you for the last four years of discipleship—for challenging me to contemplate my ways of thinking and expecting me to confidently live out my beliefs. Thank you for the countless hours of conversations about how God is interacting with us, teaching us, and encouraging us. I am deeply thankful for you and the inspiration you have been to me. See you all in the Kingdom.

To the women who have invested in my life: Savannah, Grace, Caroline, Kimberly, Jessica, Sarah, and Angie. Thank you for believing in me and guiding me. Your humility and kindness have refined my harsh edges and shaped me into a more gracious and empowered woman. Thank you for sharing some of your secrets between you and God with me. I truly admire your faith. Your faithfulness inspires me. You'll always have an open door to my world.

To My Girls,

I don't know how this book found its way into your hands. Maybe you picked it up at a Little Free Library or found an anonymous package on your front porch. For however this book made its way to you, I'm thankful. But I'm even more thankful that you are here. I hope this book accompanies you as you curl up in a cozy chair with a warm drink or lay out in the sun with an ice-cold refreshment. No matter the season, I want to show you ways to live a more abundant life in Christ.

I bet you've been hurt, felt stuck, or gotten knocked off track before. You might feel broken or directionless. You may even feel like you're just trying to get through this part of life to some "greener grass" somewhere, someday. But you don't have to wait. I'm here to supply you with tools to cultivate a life full of wonder and beauty right now. I want to lead you to the peaks of power within you and guide you through an exploration of your inherent value.

My life has flourished over the last few years—not because it's been easy but because God has taught me more of His kindness and nearness. I've been able to see the growth of the girls I've discipled as they learn more about God as well. I want that kind of transformation for you, too.

None of this growth is sustainable without love, so we're not going to stray away from that focus. Part one of the book takes you into a deeper knowledge of God as you explore loving God. You'll discover more about God as a living Being who wants a relationship with you, the ways you most comfortably connect with Him, and how you can challenge yourself to spend time with Him in new ways. The second part of the book guides you toward inner peace through learning how to love yourself. You'll wrestle with hope for a blessing, find freedom in your limitations, and become a champion of rest. The third part of the book prepares you to launch out into the world by empowering you to love others. You'll learn what it takes to influence places and people for the better through the liberating love in you.

I can't promise you that I can give you an abundant life, but I don't have to. Jesus already did. I want to lead you back again and again to His invitation for the thirsty to drink of everlasting life and be filled. I want to encourage you to not give up and to not glide through Christianity. You are a miracle to this world, and I'm here to help you discover the miracles you are capable of. I want to walk you into the glory you were made for.

The best kind of life I can show you is a life of extravagant love. You can always be transformed by love, no matter where your starting point is. My prayer for you is that by the time you reach the end of this book, you will feel more immersed in the love of God, and that love will strengthen you and overflow into the lives around you. I cannot wait for you to experience the nurturing and pruning of the Gardener—partaking in His efforts to make your life beautiful.

Love,

Savannah

Contents

Introduction

Before ascending to the right hand of the Father, Jesus' final words were "Go make disciples" (Matthew 28). Sharing His teachings with others was not meant to be a specific calling for specific people. It is an invitation to transform the way we live, which inevitably transforms the lives of those around us. Discipleship isn't dutiful drudgery or a competitor with our careers— it's love lived out. It's what Christianity was always meant to be —Jesus' friends loving each other and leading others to love Him too.

As we lead others to follow Jesus, we teach them what Jesus taught us so they can disciple others to do the same. This is how we spread Gospel with a solid foundation—not by building a following but by following Jesus together. The beauty of discipleship is the glory of God evident in our love for one another. That beauty has adorned the last few years of my life and inspired me to give generously in the way others have given to me.

Discipleship has changed my life in the ways I've grown to love God, myself, and others. I had no idea how much more abundance was available to me until I saw my world through someone else's eyes and began hearing testimonies of what God was doing in theirs. My most impactful experience with discipleship began at the University of Georgia Wesley Foundation. UGA Wesley is a college campus ministry with a discipleship program that pairs older staff and students with younger staff and students to seek the Kingdom of God together.

Before discipleship, I was chronically anxious and endured occasional depressive episodes. For all my self-righteousness, I still held onto shame like a secret friend. I knew and loved God, but I was still searching for belonging. Years later, through what

I learned in discipleship, my life isn't run by anxiety, and I'm surrounded by friends who encourage me when I'm facing difficult times. They call out my self-righteousness when I'm acting high and mighty, and I have grown in humility enough to genuinely thank them for it. I don't feel bound to shame when I mess up because I've come to believe the love of Jesus has set me free from condemnation. I feel wanted. I'm alive with purpose within and outside of what I do. I've known the Bible thoroughly and walked with God as long as I can remember. But it was through others that He taught me how much more freedom was available for me.

I began this transformation by recognizing I am known by God and sustained by connection with Him to live well. That knowledge led me to experience greater hope for my future, acceptance of my limitations, and enjoyment of my day-to-day life. I began to live better because I was believing better about God, myself, and the world. I found the freedom to confidently advocate for the lives of people to be transformed like I was by God's grace and love expressed through discipleship.

I'll never forget one moment after I had fully given myself to discipleship for several months when my discipler looked at me and said, "God shows up for you." We recounted the nights I spent in tears, the highs I spent in worship, and the confidence I had grown in prayer. The truth was overwhelmingly evident: God shows up for me. When I feel waves of anxiety, God is stronger than my fears. When I struggle with depression, God is a better friend than my somber thoughts. When I am thriving, God celebrates me with a shower of blessings. He is entirely faithful to me. Without my discipler, Kimberly, investing in my life through listening, challenging, and caring, I may have entirely missed how God was teaching me more about His love for me.

This is one of many testimonies I've experienced and witnessed through discipleship. God knew what He was doing when He gave us one another. There is no struggle, no brokenness, no fear that cannot be conquered and healed through Jesus. One of the best parts of following Jesus is that you don't have to do it alone. I was—and still am—refined through the discipleship of Jesus and the people who have helped guide me. The encouragement and accountability of discipleship leads me into a fuller life that pleases God. Becoming disciples of Jesus was God's idea, so we know it's good. It's not until we join in that we get to experience how great it is.

Inspired by the women who invested in my spiritual growth throughout college and working in ministry, I decided to follow in their footsteps and disciple younger girls as well. My first three sophomores immediately stole my heart. Beyond the nervous excitement and awkward silences, my heart burst with hope for all God might do in and through them. Each girl that joined my discipleship group filled me with gratitude and a sense of wonder that God created her, was with her in every moment of her life, and had even more goodness for her than she had experienced before. I witnessed miracle after miracle through their vulnerability and testimonies. They pushed me with their questions about God and life, challenged me to live up to my beliefs, and inspired me to write this book.

This book exists to help you grow, to accompany you through whatever stage of life you're in, and to remind you that you are loved. The content is drawn from conversations with my disciplers and my girls. Whether you've been discipled by someone for years or you're still looking for someone to invest in your spiritual growth, my desire is that this book can enhance your growth as you become like Jesus.

Aaron Vickroy, the director of discipleship at Wesley, once spoke to the staff about "favorites." He suggested the term doesn't always carry a negative connotation of comparison or privilege, but could simply describe "people of favor" the same way "Israelites" describes "people of Israel." Aaron encouraged us to give favor to the people we discipled so they can bless the people around them. What I saw in each one of my disciplers was the favor they gave me—the extra time, the intentional conversations, the special care they treated me with. My girls freely have my favor because they are the ones God has blessed me with, and that is the way God has shown love to me.

Now I invite you to be one of my girls—to enjoy this intentionally crafted labor of love, to grow from the knowledge I've gained through my own relationship with God, and to receive the blessings of all the prayers I've been praying for you. I believe you will live a more wild and free life as you discover how loving God, yourself, and others can create miracles.

Part I: Loving God

"We love God because He first loved us." 1 John 4:19

Known

In the very beginning, God created humanity. Our history starts with God's desire for us. Our relationship with God began before He even created us. Seeking a greater knowledge of God is a worthwhile, steadfast pursuit. He loves us. He is more endless and unknown than the depths of the sea or space. How could I ever give up on exploring such an endeavor? Those small glimpses of enlightenment when Scripture makes sense are unparalleled experiences.

When I first arrived at college, I began to understand the value of knowing myself. I used to think it didn't matter for me to know myself. The notion was confusing to me: How could I not know me? I am me. Then I joined a campus ministry where the staff inspired me to consider how well I really knew myself; they had confidence in the unique ways they were made and had love for one another that I had not seen in other ministries.

As I built relationships with some of the staff members, I began to notice the trend of how each person embraced his or her unique qualities. They could tell me their strengths, their purposes, their dreams with little-to-no hesitation. With their support guiding me, I dove into prayerful self-discovery. I wrote out my testimony to find themes in my life. I discovered my strengths and God-given abilities. I created a mission statement for my life and a declaration of identity: "I am known and delighted in by our gracious God who is making me beautiful, leading me in abundant life, and sustaining me with the fullness of joy from His Spirit dwelling in me."

My friends came alongside me in the process to help me understand more about my leadership style and the ways I am perceived by others. I used countless pages in my journal and notes app on my phone to ask God what He thinks about me or how He is developing me then record His responses. Rather than using my growing insight about myself to bolster my pride, I found pathways to humility. Recognizing the individuality of myself and others has produced more awe in me for the Creator.

Being made in the likeness of an infinite God, I believe we reflect attributes of the infinite God into our finite world. I have more confidence in my identity and more enjoyment in my life because I know who God is and who He created me to be. That's the kind of confidence and joy I want for you, too.

Made with Purpose
My eternal purpose is to be loved by God. So is yours. Do you ever wonder why you're here? You're wanted. You're desired. You're loved. Love can be the foundation for us as we explore who God is, who we are, and how to live abundantly. Experiential knowledge is as valuable as informational knowledge when it comes to knowing Him because we've been created with a purpose that can only be fulfilled through receiving the love of God. Be loved. We were made by God for God (Colossians 1:16).

We don't pursue God because it's our responsibility but because He is our source of life. He is the Vine; we are the branches (John 15:5-8). Connected to Him, we will feel the greatest sense of purpose and enjoyment of life. I am a dwelling place for the Holy Spirit so I am most alive when I feel Him with me. That's when I am living exactly as I was made to live.

Without a doubt, you have dreams and a purpose. You have the influence to bring some dreams to reality. He will lead us on incredible journeys that will bless others because He asks us to love the world with integrity and honor. He did it first when God became a man and displayed the greatest measure of love—laying down His life for us. Now we have the ability to do the same. And as we do the same, others will gain the authority to do the same in their circles. And so on. The Great Commission wraps up everything Jesus taught on earth and hands it to us as a gift to give away to everyone: "Go show the world My love." God intends for us to live well; He has made so much available to us for us to enjoy and share with others.

The truth in Revelation 1:5-6 can change your life: "To him who loves us and has freed us from our sins by His blood, and has made us to be a kingdom and priests to serve his God and Father…" John, the writer of Revelation, is saying this to the seven Churches in Asia right before they get called out for abandoning the love they had at first, holding fast to false teachings, seducing servants of God to sexual immorality, having a reputation of being alive when they're dead inside, and, essentially, pride. This makes me think that no one is disqualified from the inheritance they have in Jesus when they begin to hear what the Spirit is saying and respond in obedience. We don't need to shy away from who He has created us to be. We can embrace the holiness God has washed us in.

You are loved. You are free from sin. We were made for what were traditionally the most royal and holy occupations. Now that you've found purpose, let's discover your individuality.

Uniquely Made

I began an investigation of generational blessings a few years ago. I had heard the term before in different ministry settings and quietly dismissed it as an idea restricted to the Old Covenant in the Old Testament. I still believe we are new creations in Christ, but I have since recognized factors that I believe support the notion of generational blessings.

Generational blessings are essentially products of sowing and reaping (Galatians 6:8). My great-grandmother sowed into her relationship with God, and my grandma reaped. Then my grandma sowed into her relationship with God, and my mother reaped. My mother sowed into her relationship with God, and now I reap the fruit of hers as I sow into mine with God. The blessing my great-grandmother reaped and released for generations was a desire to know God.

I have been generationally blessed. My parents are incredible people. They have been following the Lord since long before I was born and continue to walk with Him day by day. I would be foolish to think that their relationships with God have not affected my own. By some miracle, I have been developing a personal relationship with God since I was a child. I don't recall a specific moment when I decided to deviate from their ways of relating to God and establish my own. However, I am confident that, as I grew up, I eventually developed my own relationship with God apart from my parents. Their prayers and guidance set me on a path I don't want to get off.

My dad has been involved in ministry for my entire life. I can just tell that he was made for it. If he weren't ministering the way he feels led by God to, he wouldn't be fully living the way he was intended to live when God first dreamed of him. My dad teaches with more wisdom and accuracy than most speakers I've ever heard. I trust his knowledge of the Bible's context, references, and interpretations more than any other resource.

Apart from his vocation, he is a man of integrity and deeply family-oriented. He demonstrates what it means to live in obedience to God as depicted in John 15. He is open to correction, unwavering in devotion, quick to apologize, and slow to get angry. He reminds me that prayer is enjoyable and worship is never a waste of time through his words and his lifestyle. He loves to laugh and care for people like they are his own. He's intentional with his close relationships and proud to say when he is proud of them.

In more recent years, I have watched him fall in love with Jesus all over again as if it were the first time. He represents the never-ending and ever-increasing love of God that is available to me. He hears God and speaks with humility. He allows God to transform him from glory to glory at His will. My dad is powerful and important, and I would not be the same without him.

My mom is everything beautiful. She's one of those winsome people that others are attracted to by some ineffable quality. I think it has something to do with her bubbly and gracious nature, but there is also a quieter spiritual draw to who she is that leads people in Kroger or the gas station to strike up a conversation with her out of nowhere. She is the foremost prophetic voice in my life. Legalism is shattered in her presence because she overcame that long before I was born, and now she sets an example of radical love toward people. She is hospitable, generous, and lives abundantly every day as if it were the greatest adventure with God available. She taught me to be still before the Lord and to be real before the Lord.

Her life is a pursuit of growth because learning brings her joy. Striving for perfection is not on her radar because becoming like God is natural for someone who spends her life looking at God. My favorite compliment I receive is when people tell me that I am like my mom. She's wild, fun, and emotional in all the best ways. She reminds me that it's okay to grieve and be angry because our hope in God is strong enough to carry us through any heartache. She effortlessly demonstrates the sacrificial love of the Father and the comfort of the Holy Spirit. My mom is powerful and important, and I would not be the same without her.

As an offspring of these two superhumans, I have learned and received from them for over twenty years and counting. Because of them, I love the Word of God and the place of prayer. I can spend hours worshipping and still want more. I can create family with those God has placed in my life and be an example of how fun life is with God. I realize I am blessed to have the parents I have.

Not everyone has parents who set a good and godly example of living for them. I have many close friends who haven't experienced the same gift of spiritual guidance that I have. I believe this is unjust—never part of the reality our Father intended for His children. But spiritual parents are not limited to biological parents. I have many leaders I submit to and learn from that are related and unrelated. My sister, my discipler, and leaders from different ministries all have unique voices in my life. "There is safety in having many advisors" (Proverbs 11:14 NLT), and even my friends with unsatisfying parent-child relationships have found ways to receive blessings from the leaders in their lives.

A man named Clay Kirkland founded the ministry internship program at the University of Georgia Wesley Foundation where I worked for three years. He taught me about leading well. He advised us to appoint people in our lives like Jethro from Exodus 18. We should allow a trusted, wise person to speak into our plans and decisions with freedom. An outside perspective from a loving friend will call us higher and remind us of what is available to us. We should identify the people who see the best in us and ask them to push us toward that version of ourselves.

Another leader, Blake Wiggins, taught me to call out the gold in people—to ask for God's opinion of a person and encourage them with whatever truth we sense God speaking over them. He instilled truth in us that prophecy doesn't entitle us to judge the faults of people in the name of God, but the gift of the Spirit empowers us to call out the good in them and build them up in love. He often spoke of Matthew 10:41-42 about receiving a prophet or a righteous man for who he is, and, in turn receiving the blessing of that man. He challenged us to see the best in people, give people the space to be their best selves, and receive the blessing they are through that.

By receiving someone who is gentle-spirited, I give them permission to be gentle-spirited around me and get to witness the wonder of them living in their most authentic identity. I can learn from them how to be gentle as well. If I didn't receive the person and accept their gentleness, I would miss out on the beauty that person has to offer the world and probably make that person feel insignificant. By receiving someone who is extremely bold, I can give them permission and space to be bold. I'll get to watch their wild life unfold that I may have otherwise run from. In beholding their victories, I can become braver myself.

Ask God about the people in your life and what makes them unique. We don't need to change them. We need to find the good in them, receive the good from them, and encourage the good we've seen in them. We can learn from them. One of my spiritual fathers asked me what role I needed him to play in my life because I already have so many incredible leaders to look up to. After prayer, I realized that I just needed him to be him because no one else could fill that role in my life. I think that's what the world needs from me, too. We can simply receive people for who they are.

I want to be uniquely me so the people around me can receive what I have to offer and give it away. I need to remain rooted in the Word and full of joy in the presence of God because that's what I know I was created for. Then the ones who see my passion for the Word and persistent joy can see that it's possible to live the same way and pursue those qualities for themselves. Others will be impacted by their lives, and the ripple effect will go beyond what I will see this side of eternity. The world needs us to be who God created us to be and for us celebrate one another's individuality. That's how we build up the Church and become more like Christ. God never intended for us to stay the same. He created us to evolve from glory to glory into the likeness of Jesus. But we will never step into all that is available to us without forgiveness.

Freedom in Forgiveness
Forgiveness is a key I've found to unlock my potential, par-

ticularly when it comes to breaking patterns of learned behavior and combating genetic predispositions. There's a concoction of addiction, anxiety, and depression running through my DNA. As I forgive my lineage for succumbing to these struggles, I can lead in freedom from it all. When we can let go of things that people have said or done that damaged us, we can receive good from them. We'll learn lessons as we shift our perspective from bitterness to forgiveness. It is a life prayer of mine that my heart is not hardened. I want to be sensitive to what God is saying, what I am feeling, and what the people around me might be experiencing so that I can fully participate in life.

I like to ask God to search my heart and see if there's any offensive way in me often, like David did, trusting that He'll convict me so I don't have to condemn myself. In one of these "come to Jesus" moments, I realized I was carrying the weight of instructions my parents had ingrained into my conscience. "Immediately, completely, without complaining" was the communicated, expected response when they asked me to do something. This is wise and beneficial counsel for building relationships, honoring God well, and functioning effectively later in life. But having it said over and over throughout my childhood made me build an immunity to the intended heart behind it. While my parents were hoping I would learn to respond to people and situations promptly, engaged, and thankful, I eventually registered it as a robotic response to any request.

In order to see myself the way God sees me, as a living being, I had to forgive myself for misinterpreting a phrase my parents were only using to develop me into a capable adult. God doesn't desire for me to respond in a heartless, quick way. He wants my heart, soul, mind, and strength. I accepted His invitation to release that lie and live in the intended blessing of the instruction. This kind of redemption is available for all sorts of misinterpretations.

My dad called me "doll" growing up, and I grew resentful toward the term of endearment the older I got. I couldn't hear it without feeling pressured to be a picture-perfect, well-behaved, quiet daughter. Of course that was never his intention, but I was used to carrying that weight of expectation to "honor" him.

I told him it bothered me in high school, and he stopped. In later years, I missed the expression. It took a long time, but I finally realized his intentions behind it. I could have accepted that he was calling me beautiful like God does, but instead I twisted into something it wasn't. Don't let offense steal away what God has spoken over you. Release those phrases and names; ask God to redeem them. Years after that confrontation with my dad, a woman approached me in the back of a church and told me I looked pretty as a doll. It was a special moment between me and God because I could finally receive it as a compliment. I called my dad and told him how thankful I was for the care with which he raised me.

Forgiveness for my own misunderstandings and for others' clears the fog of selfish ambition so I can walk forward in love. With this gift from God, you can confidently take steps toward your purpose.

Finding Your Path

A lot of students I've talked to have wondered what major to choose or which career path to take because they don't want to miss God's calling for their lives. Worrying about the future is a common distraction when we are faced with forks in the road. According to 2 Thessalonians 2:14, we are called to share in the glory of God. 2 Timothy 1:9 says we are called to live a holy life. 1 Corinthians 1:9 says we are called into relationship with the Son. When I look through the Bible, I find that we are called to love God and be loved by Him. Like Father, Son, and Spirit, we join in the unity of perfect love. That calling is your calling. We received access to that unity when we received Christ. Go after that and everything else will be added to you (Matthew 6:33). Seek that, and you won't miss out on what God has for you.

I've never missed God's plans while following Him because He is kind. He's not withholding or misleading. Our callings are to live with eternal mindsets and love big because we are loved. Proverbs 16:9 says, "in their hearts humans plan their course, but the Lord establishes their steps." We can plan, we can dream, and we can believe God will establish our steps. He did not intend for us to live in anxiety. I've found anxiety to be the greatest waste of my time and brain power. He has assured us that He will take care of what is to come.

There are times in Scripture that God calls specific people to do specific things, and what I've noticed about those testimonies is that the people who are called don't miss their callings. It's not a hidden mystery they have to figure out on their own. God

9

makes their paths apparent and makes a way for them. Take the pressure off yourself to walk on a specific path. If God wants something for you, and you're choosing Him daily, you don't have to live with the fear you're going to "miss it." He's not keeping secrets from you to make you mess up. If you're directly defying His calling, you can trust Him to show you. He reproves those He loves (Revelation 3:19). He'll keep you on track as you follow Him.

God tells us what's important to Him for us to do: abide in love, make disciples, give to the poor, care for the oppressed, etc. You can do that however and in any place God leads you to. The rest of your life is up to the dreams you create with God. It's never too late. Hope big and ask big. Pray for favor and watch opportunities show up. Then take them and run. When those end, start again. There's so much life to live. What does it look like to live for more? There's life where you are, right in front of you. What opportunities are in reach? Oftentimes a change of perspective is all you need to find your next step.

God dreamed of us before we were in our mothers' wombs; He knit us together. His thoughts toward us outnumber the grains of sand in existence, and He calls us altogether beautiful (Psalm 139). We are intentional creations. Every person has something to offer. Even if it seems similar to someone else, it cannot be. We are an assortment of our experiences, genes, gifts, passions, and dreams. No one could be or should be a carbon copy of anyone else.

We shouldn't hold back who we are. We should know ourselves and be ourselves. What would the world look like if we each chased our potential? Once, I attended Cirque du Soleil with my family and some friends, and we were blown away by the talent. All of a sudden, I felt overwhelmed by the beauty of the performance. I wondered to myself what it took for these unbelievably skilled humans to stretch their limits as far as they had. How many nights had they spent dreaming? How many hours had they spent pushing themselves? I got to see everything that I would have otherwise missed out on if any of them had given up. We don't really know what we are capable of until we begin pushing ourselves.

There's a universe inside of each of us. I could spend my whole life getting to know myself and always be surprised. I am always changing, always growing—and so are you. We will adapt to our surroundings, our loved ones, and our new under-standings as we age. This is nothing to be afraid of. Sometimes when I coach people in Emotional Intelligence, I tease them that they could be entirely different people in six months when I follow up with them. I know as they put effort into developing their soft skills, they will achieve the results they want. We may be familiar to our future selves, but we will not be the same. Think of who you were five years ago. Are you the same today or have you changed? Was the change worth it? Are you stronger now? Every moment of your life has contributed to making you more unique, more beautiful, more you. And you are going to live for-ever.

Eternity

Since I was young I remember having the conviction that I was made for eternity. My dad taught me to have an eternal per-spective in his classes and in the home. He encouraged us to live with the knowledge that we are living beyond what we know in this life. This life is fleeting and momentary. Eternity with God is our everlasting home.

Heaven is talked about in many different ways. It's a city, a garden, a throne room, mansions, and paradise. I think these are all parts of the amazing environment for our everlasting spirits. We were made for a redeemed earth in which there is no dark-ness. God is the light of the city, which means there's no hiding, no shame, and no fear in the night. It is a renewed creation in which there is no pain and every tear is wiped away.

Healing and the fullness of joy are natural and available. No one will be married or given in marriage like we know now. We are the Bride of Christ, together with all the saints, and we will celebrate our love for God forever. It doesn't seem real, but let me challenge you to start imagining that you have an upcoming wedding. To God. After you die.

We were made for a heavenly city so far beyond our wildest dreams. We weren't made for a world that is broken and full of sin. That was never God's pure intention for our lives. He wanted to be in communion with us as we exercise authority over all that is created. Even the best life on earth now is only a shadow of the life to come. Eternity is written on our hearts (Ecclesiastes 3), which I believe is why we struggle to feel satisfied with the way this world turns. We were made for one so much better.

The entrance to eternal life is Jesus Christ. The most important thing to remember is that God is what gives eternal life value. The Father sent His Son to make a way for us to be with Him, which is why it is vital to believe the words of Jesus about who the Father is and to let the Spirit guide you into all truth. Our goodness cannot merit enough righteousness to stand before the Holy God. We are invited into everlasting life with pleasures evermore (Psalm 16:11) by the grace of God through faith in Christ (Ephesians 2:8).

When we know God, we love God; when we love God, we worship. That's why eternity is filled with worship. We will get to see Him for who He is and be overwhelmed. Maybe we'll sing "holy" for the rest of our days like the creatures in Revelation 4. Maybe we'll cast down God-given crowns before His throne like the elders in the same passage. Maybe we'll stand with multitudes—thousands upon thousands—singing in every language of the great and marvelous works of God. I think this is why learning to enjoy worship is so important on this side of death. Worship is what we will do for all eternity, and we'll love it.

When Jesus talked about storing up treasures in heaven, I don't think He was joking (Matthew 7). I believe there will be treasures for us in the life to come, just like He promised in His Word. Even the devotion you displayed for God in secret will be rewarded openly there. He has explicitly communicated His generosity intended for us all throughout Scripture and He's not One to go back on His Word.

Knowing our lives extend beyond this temporal one propels us into more extravagant lives—not to waste or boast but to love and serve. We are citizens of a Kingdom so different from what we can see in government across the world today. We can pursue callings and vocations as avenues to exercise the gifts God has given us already. We don't have to settle for chasing promotions, raises, and titles.

Don't Settle

I've seen the temptation to settle for less than what we were created for in many students and friends. The worst is seeing it up close and personal. The core of what I have learned in the last few years is that God is good. Settling is never the plan for us. We were made with purpose.

Clay, who I mentioned earlier, had a phrase he was credited

with because he would use it so often: "No pressure, just opportunity." The words release a person from obligation and into invitation. For example, Clay would ask different people to pray to close out each staff meeting. The question "Would you like to close us out in prayer?" has a social pressure attached to it. But following the request with "No pressure, just opportunity" offers the option to fill the request out of willingness instead of duty. This phrase has freed me from false expectations and provided an invitation to achieve with more joy and autonomy than I knew were available to me.

When Clay first heard the phrase, the man who said it had also added, "You're wonderful." I think the two phrases paired together are so powerful. I find freedom when I realize that I am wonderful. God created me fearfully and wonderfully (Psalm 139). This is not pride but a joyful alignment with truth. Further freedom comes when I realize there is no pressure on my life, just opportunity.

Jesus died for us to choose him. Freedom and love come with that choice. Control is linked with fear. I don't believe Jesus is controlling our lives—that He's set one career for us and, if we miss out on it, we miss out on God. Although God is sovereign, I can't say my knowledge of Scripture supports that "God is in control" in the sense that He is controlling. He is capable and all-powerful, but so much of His expression of love is laying down His life. I believe He is sovereign and that He is with us. He directs our steps and has hope for us. He has made opportunities for us that we would never dream of apart from Him. We know that God does greater than what we ask or imagine.

God, Himself, is greater than we ask or imagine (Ephesians 3:20). I have been guilty of settling in who I know God to be. I'll go for days, weeks, sometimes months at a time without a curiosity stirring in me to know more about our infinite God. Job says, "How great is God—beyond our understanding! (Job 36:26)." I think I could seek God my whole life and still repeat that phrase with my dying breath. He's more fun, more powerful, more complex than we often acknowledge. The knowledge we gain about God, both informational and experiential, can change the way we live. If we base our perception of God off of our current information and experiences, we will come up short.

God is greater than our limited experiences. Know Him beyond what you know. We can trust him beyond our understanding (Proverbs 3). Don't settle for what you've seen and heard. Taste and see that He is good, then earnestly seek Him more. A hunger for more of God is the most exciting dissatisfaction you can experience because He fills the hungry with good things (Psalm 107:9).

Not settling means clinging to a lot of hope and a lot of patient endurance as we press on toward Christ. Knowing we were made for more than the lives we are currently living is enchantingly inspiring—until we are faced with people close to us who don't believe in us or we are challenged with seemingly endless setbacks. Not settling means choosing contentment in all things, too. Strange as it sounds, it actually makes sense. As we pursue more of God, more for ourselves, more for those around us, we must learn to be content with what God is doing. Otherwise we will strive in frustration instead of love as our motivation. Not settling means knowing we are worthy of love. You are worthy of love. Begin picturing your life with that truth as the foundation.

Dream a Little

The first step in living for all you were made to is to dream about what you might be made for. In an imagination without limitation, who are you? Who is your ideal self? I like to list out what I want to see in my future. I hold them loosely, but they are things I work toward. The list includes characteristics I hope to see in career possibilities, future relationships, places I'd like to live or visit, and qualities I aspire to possess myself. Writing helps us have something to refer to when we feel less hopeful about our lives and futures, but it also helps our brains in the process of forming long-term memories for our goals. Writing forces us to seriously consider the dreams we've created for our lives and the steps we must take to reach them.

> What are twenty things you would like to see happen in your life?

> What are twenty things you would like to happen through you?

> What are twenty things you want to accomplish?

These are all stepping stones to a more adventurous future. Some things could be completely fantastic and some can be shortly attainable. Get your mind turning about what you're moving toward. Practical advice I've received from a few friends is to never make a decision out of fear.

What would you change today if you weren't afraid?

What would you do if you were a little bolder?

The answer to these questions can fill your dream world and give you a vision for where you could be headed in life. I like to ask myself who is living like I want to live and what makes their lives so attractive to me. I can look at the ways other individuals in my lifetime have done the things I aspire to do and find ways to make aspects of my life similar to theirs. I love that Bob Goff writes books, teaches, and provides aid in Uganda, so I have modeled my approach to life after his. I write when I get the chance, teach when I get the chance, and minister in every opportunity I can find. I will never be Bob Goff, nor should I be, but I can adopt the admirable qualities of his life to enhance my own experiences.

One of my leaders asked me what I want to have defined my life when I'm at the end of it. I thought about what I want to be a part of in my lifetime and what I would like to accomplish. All these dreams I have brought before God. I trust Him to bring it all together, open doors, and do more than I've imagined for myself. For the dreams that will someday be realized, I am grateful; for the dreams that will never happen, I trust God will do something better. And I know God will bring pieces of my life together that are even better than I ever dreamed. He's that good.

The Character of God

After Jesus teaches us about abiding in love and the Holy Spirit in John, He begins to address the Father saying, "This is eternal life: that they know you, the only true God, and Jesus Christ whom you sent." At the end of His prayer, He promises to make the Father known in order that the love the Father has for Jesus may be in us as well (John 17). Jesus was on a mission for us to know the Father. Then, when He left, He left us with the Spirit who reveals the Father and searches the deepest parts of

15

the Father's heart (1 Corinthians 2:10). The knowledge of God is everything. Both experiential knowledge and informational knowledge add to our grasp at understanding and living in eternal life.

God is far beyond my comprehension of Him. I've known of His love since infancy, and still I learn of His love. I have minuscule knowledge of His glory, and yet I know He is glorious. His goodness and mercy unfold before me more and more day by day, but I've barely begun to understand His nature. Building a stronger foundation in comprehending God's character is a never-ending project. God is infinite but not out of reach. His character is an easy place to begin the journey of knowing Him more because it's riddled in Scripture and reflected in His children.

We waste our lives on empty religion if we don't truly know God. Christianity is no more than a moral guideline for living contrived from an attempt to explain the purpose and origin of life if we extract knowing God from it; really, that's not Christianity at all. Christians—followers of Christ—are those committed to knowing the Father because that's what Jesus was committed to.

What does God mean to you? How do you relate to Him? What do other people seem to know about Him that you want to know for yourself? These are all catalyst questions into the most fantastic and wonderful exploration of a Being.

Lucky for us, God's character is so good that we can trust anything we learn about Him will show us He is better than we had known before, not worse. I've had conversations with students who were afraid that if they pull on a string of God's character, the whole fabric of their knowledge of God will come undone. If it does, good. There's some better truth they were missing out on that they now know they can discover.

I find we are guilty of asking God the questions that He's asking us. We turn questions around on Him because we don't trust His character. My girls have asked me, "How can God be good if someone suddenly passed away, and I didn't even get to say goodbye?" or "Why won't God just tell me where to go next in life instead of letting me worry?" or "Why does God speak to other people and not me?" These are great questions to be asking; we just don't need to make them rhetorical.

When I was grieving the death of a loved one, I asked God for days why He would let that happen. In my silent anger, I felt

God ask me the same question back. "Why do you think I would let that happen?"

I began furiously journaling in search of truth. Did God let that happen? Did He make it happen? Is He really good? Is He really sovereign? What I found after journaling for two days was enough to let me feel peace and trust God again. Yes, He is sovereign. The Bible says so. Yes, He is good. I have experienced His goodness and so have generations before me. I don't know if He made the loss happen or let it happen, but I know that He was compassionate toward me in my grief. And I believe that He was thrilled to have my loved one with Him at long last. I had to get to the point in which I understood my circumstances through the knowledge of God's character rather than letting my knowledge of my circumstances determine my understanding of God's nature. His character is sovereign, good, compassionate, and loving. The nature of God trumps everything. He is Truth. His character is immutable.

If our theology does not account for the living nature of God, then it will never be accurate. Our theology cannot be focused on being a good person and doing good deeds because it's never been about our goodness but His. I want to challenge you to know the living God and step into eternal life. Know Him as Friend and Father. Are you able to list out each of His characteristics and how you have seen them like you could for a close friend? I can't list them all, but I love trying. He is gracious, and He shows me grace when I get easily frustrated by patiently calming my anger. He is kind, and He shows me kindness by clearing the skies to bring me beautiful days. He is real, and He is great. You won't be disappointed.

Dehumanizing God

I was talking to some of my good friends in the car about reading the Word. I explained what I had been learning about the importance of the Holy Spirit's role as we read His Word. This was one of those moments when I start rambling about things I believe but then I say something that is way wiser than I could give myself credit for; I couldn't have told you it before I said it. I didn't know I knew what I said until it had crossed over my lips. This simple yet new-to-me revelation was that God has thoughts and feelings that I should be curious about as I explore the Word. So often we are guilty of dehumanizing God.

Dehumanizing God is the result of lacking accurate knowledge of God. This doesn't mean we have to study more to know that God has thoughts and feelings; we only need to alter our perceptions of who He is based on the truth that He exists. We change our minds and decide to believe He is who He says He is. This is what He has said:

> He has emotions
> He loves (Romans 5:8)
> He feels angry (Psalm 106:40)
> He grieves (John 11:35)
> He rejoices (Zephaniah 3:17)
> He has thoughts (Psalm 139:17)
> He makes choices (Ephesians 1:4-5)
> He has opinions (1 Timothy 2:3-4)

God desires connection with us. Often a barrier to our relationship with God is failure to acknowledge that God is alive. When I believe God is always angry, boring, or distant, I disconnect because eternal negative emotion is not something I was created for. I was created through God for God who is love (Colossians 1:16; 1 John 4:16). When I come into alignment with truth, I understand that God kind, generous, and good. He is a living Being.

I was meditating on Matthew 26:7: "a woman came to [Jesus] with an alabaster jar of very expensive perfume, which she poured on his head while he was reclining at the table." Forty-five minutes into exploring the depths of this verse and writing down the implications for my life, I realized that expensive perfume was poured onto flesh. Jesus was feeling and smelling this pleasing fragrance. He was being ministered to and cared for. Based on the event and His response, I think Jesus felt loved in this moment. How often in Jesus' lifetime on earth do you see someone selflessly loving Him? She honored Him when He was reclining at the table.

As far as we know, He had not done anything at that moment to earn her affection, He just was being. He had raised her brother from the dead some time before that, so she had experienced his goodness in the past. But then and there, He rested as she showered affection on Him. I imagine in that moment Jesus felt the Father's love interwoven with her offering of appreciation.

The woman in this passage didn't use her moment with Jesus to ask for healing, answers, or provision; she used it to minister to Him. Many times in Scripture I see Jesus heal, answer, and provide what was in accordance with the will of the Father (John 5:19). But this is a time Jesus was resting and still in accordance with the will of the Father. I would suggest that God's rest is not to distance Himself from us but to extend an invitation for the exchange of mutual affection without pressure or expectation, only the extravagance of love and honor.

I know He is Healer, Teacher, and Provider. I can trust that He will do all that He wants to do in His own timing. When He rests, I can serve without feeling forced and unappreciated. I can come close without feeling like I'm intruding or He is exhausted of me. I can minister to God and so can you—welcome to the holy priesthood (Revelation 1:6). Reflecting on my own moments with God, I've realized that when I feel His presence resting on me, I don't feel a need for anything more. He is everything I need; He is more than enough. He satisfies my soul. His presence is fullness of joy, peace that passes understanding, and unconditional love. Abiding in those moments makes my joy complete (John 15:11). Moments come in which I need God to work, and He does. But I don't want to miss out on the moments resting with God because I have begun to think of God as a machine rather than a Being.

I don't want to dehumanize God any more than I would try to remove His divinity from my understanding of Him. He is holier than I am with more glory and majesty than I can fully know right now (1 Corinthians 13:9). But I cannot allow the mystery of who He is to prohibit me from pursuing the knowledge of Him. What I do not understand is an invitation to wonder and understand by the work of the Holy Spirit in me.

Jesus is fully God and fully man, fulfilling the law and the prophets. This includes a particularly relevant verse from Leviticus 26 that says:

> "I will put my dwelling place among you, and I will not abhor you. I will walk among you and be yoru God, and you will be my people. I am the Lord your God, who brought you out of Egypt so that you would no longer be slaves to the Egyptians; I broke the bars of your yoke and enabled you to walk with heads held high."

In this passage, God is revealing that He has made a place to rest among us, He has emotions, He walks among us, He is our God, we are His, He is Lord, He delivers, we are no longer slaves, He has freed us, and we can walk in freedom. That is a lot of truth for a small portion of Scripture. I hope it inspires you to meditate on the Word and pursue the knowledge of God. He is worth knowing.

We are made in the image of God. God is an emotional being, so we are emotional beings. I find it important to remember that we did not create God in our minds and therefore ascribe human attributes to a collective glorified imagination. We inherited emotions as a part of our likeness to the Father. Emotions originated from God who is good, the Source of all good, the Maker of all things good, and the Judge of what is good. Our emotions can be good when we choose to be like God in them rather than choosing to sin in them. Learning to recognize God's emotions and the things He does with them enlightens us to how we can become more like Him. I am doing myself a favor when I acknowledge that God has feelings and ways of functioning from those feelings.

God is a Person, not a debate topic. We don't need to have conversations like He's not listening or defend His reputation like He's a dead man being shamed. I don't want to argue with people about whether or not He is real; I hope they come to know the truth. But denying His existence does not cause Him to cease to exist. The knowledge we obtain of His character is meant to sustain intimacy between us and to amaze others—not to prove people wrong. Speaking the truth in love is more easily done when we remember God is present and alive; He is drawing all men to Himself and sustaining life in every one.

Sustained

I genuinely enjoy reading the Bible and worshiping. These two expressions of faith are my simplest forms of connecting with God. When I was a child, our family would start each morning with half an hour of meditation. Someone would turn on soft music and we would all sit together, Bibles and journals open. My youngest sibling was only three and my oldest nine. After pondering a verse or passage individually, we would take turns sharing what we learned. Reflecting on these mornings, I am convinced the Holy Spirit can speak to anyone—no matter how old, spiritual, or learned they may be. If we are willing to believe He will speak to us, He does. I hope everyone can enjoy the Word of God like I do; it is such a marvelous gift to us. Worship is similarly enjoyable. To sing or to bow in acknowledgement of my Savior is a faith-building exercise. The act faces me with the choice to believe He is real and He is worthy every time. The fulfillment that follows is further evidence. No one should have to feel bored in exploring the Word or praising God.

A dream of mine is to negate the lie that God isn't enjoyable by helping others love experiencing God. He is not only worthy of our attention and our worship because He is God—He is worthy because He is good, and He is near. He will draw near to us as we draw near to Him (James 4:8).

Knowing the Basics

I heard a message on the Gospel taught by Jessica Longino, the staff development director at Wesley, that amazed me. Weaving her way through Scripture from Genesis to Revelation, she presented a beautifully unique perspective of the Good News. I had never heard it quite that way before, although I was raised to know the Gospel thoroughly. I was moved to tears as she reminded us of the standard God had set, the height from which we had fallen, and the grace that exuded from Jesus' life, death, and resurrection. I was shocked; I felt as if I was hearing the Good News for the first time.

In the spring of that same year, I led a ministry trip of students to the International House of Prayer in Kansas City. We were hearing from Allen Hood, a leader there, on John 20. He told the story of the Gospel from the perspective of John and Peter. Again, my emotions were stirred deeply. This reminder of the personal relationship Jesus had developed with John and Peter changed the way I understood John's account of the death and resurrection of Christ. The room was filled with sweet sobs as we remembered together the extravagant love of God.

We can know the same story a hundred times over from the Gospels, overviews of the Word as a whole, movie adaptations, storybooks, and people's testimonies. Re-learning it through different stories only adds to each version. As John so poetically described in the first chapter of his book, "the Word became flesh." Jesus is the Gospel. We get to know Him as a story and as a person. We understand Him better when we know the Gospel better. Cherish moments when you understand Jesus in a deeper way, then experience that kind of moment a thousand times over throughout your life. In moments like these, we experience glimpses of eternity.

I was worshipping one Sunday evening in the prayer chapel at work by myself when I felt nudged to write down all those "God" moments I had experienced in my life. I noticed a conveniently-close, blank, white board in the front of the room with a marker. I began writing down memories one by one as they came to mind. Before I had finished a playlist of worship music, I had filled the entire white board. It was a holy moment of thankfulness for me, recognizing the greatness of God toward me personally.

One of the highlights of the Gospel for me is that Jesus made a way for me to get to the Father. I am now righteous before God and I am deeply loved. There's no denying it because Jesus displayed the greatest love that anyone ever could by paying my ransom. Jesus was never just a "get out of hell free" card. He ascended to the right hand of the Father where we will join Him someday. He gave us access to know the Father and to have the Spirit of God dwelling within us.

Another highlight of the Gospel is the word "saved" that James and Peter use in their letters. It's the Greek word "sozo," meaning "saved, healed, delivered, made whole, preserved." Salvation is so much more than a moment in which we become citizens of heaven. We are rescued from sin, yes. But we are also now recipients of an inheritance which includes healing and preservation. We are delivered and being made whole. All of eternity is given in small gifts to us on this side of death. We get to taste everlasting life and intimate knowledge of God before ever leaving this skin we live in because Jesus broke down the divide between the Divine and His fallen creation.

My dad recently texted me during the workday because he had a moment of insight on Genesis 1 related to Jesus being slain from the foundation of the world (Revelation 13:8). A portion of his message said:

> "In creating His friends, Jesus was at the same instant laying down His life for them. Had there not been a love so intense in His heart that He was willing to lay down His life for His creation, He would never had uttered the words, 'Let there be light.'"

Not only was this text incredibly exciting because I got to learn something new about God out of a very well known passage, but I was filled up for the day with a fresh revelation of God's love for us. The Gospel is an ever-flowing spring of life. The truth nourishes us and strengthens us for every day, any scenario, each moment.

The Gospel can mean different things at different times; I think it's important to recognize and share what it means to us with others. This is how we can encourage others in faith, learn from one another, and be witnesses to those who don't know Christ. The ultimate goal of the Gospel is to lead people into God's family. A speaker at a Christian leadership conference I attended said, "The Gospel is your story for God's glory. It's not about you." We will see ourselves in fragments of the Gospel; we are reflections of God's heart. But the entirety of the Gospel is the glory of God. He wants to show Himself to the world.

Sharing the Basics

I used to get so frustrated when I would share things God was teaching me to friends, then they would share them as if they came up with it themselves. It feels like when you say a joke quietly and no one hears it but then everyone laughs when the person next to you says it louder. Eventually, I had to come face to face with my pride and realize sharing what God is speaking is not about me—it's about Him. Actually, everything I learn from God came from God first, so I have no claim to that knowledge. I should take no pride in it. What I feel led to share with others from my relationship with God is His to disperse how He wants to. When I share what I learn with God, I get to impart that truth to strengthen others.

I have met a lot of students who feel like the Bible is difficult to understand. Breaking each phrase down into smaller pieces helps. There's no rush to get through the entire Bible. We waste time when we try to finish books instead of reading with the intent of connecting with the Spirit. Go at a pace that works for you in a method that works for you, and that's the best way you could read your Bible. As you begin to take in the bits you can, you'll be able to share those. The truth of the Word goes in through your eyes, into your heart, and out of your mouth with a little bit of your perspective tied in. I think that's part of the beauty of having access to the Word. Your experiences change the way you understand Scripture. Other people won't interpret things like you might. This is how we grow in our knowledge of God. He's bigger than our experiences. Conversations with others about verses and themes add to our perception of God and even correct our false perceptions of Him. This is one of the many ways God has revealed Himself through creation.

I've talked to students who get bored reading the Bible. I have been guilty of the same thing. "The Bible's not boring—you are" is a phrase I've grown up hearing. That doesn't change the fact that Leviticus could nearly put me to sleep, and genealogies mean next-to-nothing to me. I have to remember that I can find meaning in everything and that God was intentional about what He put in the Bible. I can learn from anything if I put in the effort. I could research the context of Leviticus or read about how genealogies have positively impacted the faith of other believers. Feeling bored is a mindset; it's our approach to what we aren't motivated to focus on. When we allow ourselves to believe the Bible is boring, we miss out on what could be an amazing learning opportunity.

If you don't know God or the Bible and want to, call a friend who does and talk to them about what they have done to mature in their faith. Try those things out. It will make the person's day, I guarantee. Then have conversations with people about what you're trying out and what you're learning.This is one of the easiest, most natural ways to make disciples. Create relationships in which you talk about God. It doesn't have to be weird. It can be your new normal, and you'll be surprised at what your life might look like in a few years when many of your relationships are centered around God. Just ask questions and listen to people. Most people have thoughts about God. See what you can learn. See what you can teach.

We waste the moments of our lives that we don't spend loving the people around us. We can share the Gospel through conversations about God but also through the actions we choose. Every breath we breathe can be a witness to the Good News. Loving well is the greatest thing we can do. We live out everything Jesus died and rose again for us to live in when we love. We bring heaven to earth, the kingdom comes, when we love. We are miracles when we love. We learn how to love by beholding Love Himself.

How to Interact with God and the Bible
Over the years of working in college ministry, I've compiled a list of ways I've interacted with God and the Bible to share with my friends, their friends, and all of our disciples. Hopefully some of what I've found useful will be helpful or at least spark creativity for your own ways of interacting. Reading the Bible and having quiet time can quickly become an empty service to God when it's so routine we hardly pay attention to what we are doing. We often find much more pleasure with God in creative approaches to our time with Him. When your Bible time feels dry, switch things up. A secret I live by is that there's no such thing as a "dry season" with God. You have a fountain of life in you because the Holy Spirit doesn't run out. So let's dive in.

Contemplative Meditation: Meditation was a part of God's desire and plan for us before it was an Eastern calming technique or pathway to enlightenment. Meditation is a discipline of attention and focus. Joshua 1:8 instructs us to meditate on the Word of God day and night. Meditation is also highly referenced and recommended throughout the Psalms. My parents introduced meditation into my Christian toolbelt when I was only seven. They had learned a method of meditation through the ministry they were a part of that I still use as a part of my regular devotions with God. We would divide the paper with two lines: one down the right side with a one-inch margin and another across the bottom of the page. We used the side margin to write down distractions and the bottom for cross-references we wanted to look at later. We would pick a single verse in the Bible and write it across the top of the page. We'd then close the Bible, remove electronics, maybe play some music in the background, and wait for God to speak as we pondered a portion of the verse on the page.

Our options in this method were to look at the Scripture and read it, write it again, sing it, say it, or pray it. It required discipline that developed over time to remain focused only on the verse at hand. I was tempted to think about what else I had to do or other aspects of God's character instead of what was in front of me. But when I chose to engage with the piece of the Word I picked, I learned how much more of God there is to discover than I knew before. Every time I meditate, I learn something new about a verse. Some verses I have meditated on dozens of times and I still receive fresh revelation each time I come back. That's the power of the living Word that is available to us. I strongly recommend starting this technique with an hour set apart. It may seem unbelievably long or unnecessary, but the students I mentor and friends I've shown who have tried it have loved it.

Creation Meditation: Creation Meditation is one method that my parents taught my siblings and I based off of Romans 1:20, which states, "For his invisible attributes, namely, his eternal power and divine nature, have been clearly perceived, ever since the creation of the world, in the things that have been made." In our application of the verse, we would go outside and pick something in creation—a tree, a leaf, a cloud, a river. Then we would set an amount of time to focus on that piece of nature and talk to God about it. I like to ask God questions like:

Why did you create this?

What does this reveal about your nature?

What does this reflect in my life?

Is this written anywhere in the Word?

Write down what you feel like God is saying in response to
your questions. Write down your thoughts and go back over
them later. Then every time you see that part of creation, you're
reminded of God. Sooner or later, wherever you look will be a
souvenir of time you spent bonding with God over His creation.
When I meditate on creation, I'm essentially living out Psalm 8:

> "When I consider your heavens, the work of your fingers,
> the moon and the stars, which you have set in place, what is
> man that you are mindful of him, the son of man that you
> care for him? You made him a little lower than the heavenly
> beings and crowned him with glory and honor. You made
> him ruler over the works of your hands; you put everything
> under his feet: all flocks and herds, and the beasts of the
> field, the birds of the air, and the fish of the sea, all that swim
> the paths of the seas. O LORD, our Lord, how majestic is
> your name in all the earth!"

It may seem strange to look for God in nature, and it could be
highly misguided if you're not also grounding yourself in Scripture. But it's actually just inviting God into another aspect of
your life and letting Him speak.

Narrative Meditation: Narrative meditation is meditating on
a passage of Scripture by inserting yourself there. Write a narrative as if you're a person mentioned in the passage or even as if
you're yourself but in that time and place. I used this when I was
doing a personal devotion time one morning before work. I had
just finished reading through my chapters of Deuteronomy for
the day. I wasn't feeling much refreshment so I opened the Bible
to Matthew 14 which shares the story of Jesus feeding the five
thousand. The chapter starts with "After this."
I wanted to know what event preceded Jesus feeding five
thousand, so I looked at the beginning Matthew 14 which tells

the story of John the Baptist's beheading. Now we know John was a relative of Jesus. When Jesus found out about John's death, He went to be alone with the Father. But by the time He stepped off the boat to find solitude, a crowd had gathered. He was filled with compassion and began healing. The disciples told Jesus it was time to go because people needed to eat, but Jesus worked a miracle and fed all of them. Jesus sent the disciples away and stayed a while longer before dismissing the crowd. Once they had all left, He was finally able to be alone and pray.

At dawn, He went back to the disciples and continued His ministry to them. This revelation was so timely and powerful for me because I was learning how to balance ministry while grieving after the death of a family member. I allowed myself to wonder what Jesus was feeling then. I imagine He was heartbroken, maybe angry. Anger may have risen up from the taste of death that He had come to free us from. I asked God how that must have hurt Him and how He dealt with the pain when there were so many people around Him who craved ministry from Him. It was a moment I connected with God because of something I was going through presently that He had gone through thousands of years before. I felt less alone in my attempts to follow God, being compassionate toward those around me in ministry while also embracing comfort from God myself.

With the Holy Spirit: Another way to read the Bible is with the Holy Spirit. This is an easy way to talk with God because the Bible is consistently "safe" to talk with God about. Sometimes I don't want to talk to God about things in my life because it's draining or I've already done it for an hour. So I grab my highlighter and ask the Holy Spirit to point things out to me. Then I start reading. Anything that sticks out to me, whether it's a word that I've been hearing a lot lately or a phrase that hits me in the soul, I highlight. One of my favorite things about reading the Bible now is flipping through colorful pages and seeing how much God has spoken to me over the years through so many different parts of the Word.

Holy Imagination: Holy Imagination is a way of connecting with God that I learned from the same man who taught my parents contemplative meditation. I had been struggling with anxiety in high school and didn't feel like there was a place I could go to find peace. So he encouraged me to close my eyes, imagine I'm in a place with God, and start interacting with Him. I won't tell you what my place is, but I will say that when I first go there, I like to imagine I'm opening a door, walking through it, and shutting it so no other thoughts can get in. It's my mental security system so I have the seclusion of just me and God. Sometimes I imagine I'm doing something with God, sometimes I imagine conversations we have. But every time, I leave with a sense of peace or joy or a truth to hold onto that I didn't have before. This is fun and can be what you make it with God. It may seem silly but we are encouraged to be childlike in our faith. God gave us imaginations. Why not use them to glorify God instead of filling them with thoughts of lust or worry or pride?

Worship: Worship is one of my secret tunnels to the presence of God. I've been privileged to work in an environment with a piano in a prayer chapel that I had access to at any time. I'd often use my free time at work to play four chords and sing whatever was on my heart. That's one of the quickest ways I can reset my emotions and will to be in alignment with God's. It's really easy to learn four chords on piano or guitar, and if you can do that, you can play almost any worship song. My favorites to play on the piano are C, Am, G, and F because there aren't any black keys involved. I've got the muscle memory now to play with my eyes closed and avoid hitting too many bad notes. It doesn't have to sound pretty for God to enjoy it and for you to meet with Him. He's a happy Father, remember? If you're not feeling excited about that, turn on worship music in the car and drive around singing your heart out. Or lay on your bed and listen to instrumental music. Write your own lyrics to God or for God. God inhabits the praises of His people (Psalm 22:3).

If a particular worship song or lyric speaks to you, go find the Scripture it's from and meditate on it. Journal about what it means to you and why the phrasing impacted you more than others. Read the context of the book it's in. This builds your knowledge of the Word and grounds you in meaningful truth. An inverse of that activity is singing the Bible. Open up the Psalms and start singing. You don't even need music. You especially don't need an audience. Just use the time to build your faith by singing to God.

Dates With God: Dates with God are so underrated. We get nervous about what other people think when we do things alone but part of faith is believing we are never alone. Dates with Him aren't anything weird or unholy. They're simply inviting God into your free time or time set apart to focus on Him. On some date nights with God, I light candles and make a cup of tea with my journal, Bible, highlighter, and pen at my disposal. Then I wait for inspiration about what to do first and do it. Once I get bored or ready to move on to the next thing, I wait for inspiration for something new and do that. And the night rolls on that way. Other times, I'll go to the free zoo in Athens and watch the bears sleep. I know God is with me (Matthew 28:20) so I just start talking to Him in my mind. You can go to the movies, you can go to dinner—do what you want. It doesn't have to be weird just because people around you don't know what's going on. You don't have to make it hyper-spiritual and talk to the empty chair across from you in a restaurant (unless you really want to).

Just invite God into a night or activity that you love and get to know Him. I live better when I live in my identity as the beloved, betrothed, bride of Christ. Going around the city with God changes the way I interact with the people I see. It even changes the way I look at them without a conversation ever happening. The nearness of God makes life better.

Praying Aloud: Praying aloud will change your prayer life. I think I'm so holy when I pray but it's not until I pray aloud that I realize how often I get distracted or run out of things to say. Vocalizing prayers so that I can hear myself speak above a whisper keeps me accountable, stirs up my passion, and increases my faith. One speaker I heard asked if faith comes by hearing, why don't we just speak things over ourselves? I don't know if Paul was trying to communicate that when he wrote Romans 10:17, "faith comes by hearing," but I'm not opposed to the bonus application of the verse. When I pray out loud on the way to work, I have a better day at work because, from the start, I'm acknowledging that God is real, present, and speaking. Most mornings, I wake up and say, "Good morning, God!" and the only ones around to hear it are me, my dog, and God. Greeting God aloud each morning serves as a reminder that He is with me and an invitation for Him to be a part of my day.

Intercession: Intercession is a form of prayer I like to engage in corporately and personally, and it's simply praying for others. We can intercede as much as we want to, agreeing with Jesus who lives to intercede for us (Hebrews 7:25). I like to write out a list (or review existing lists) of things and people I'm praying for. Then I ask God what He wants to do, how I could be praying for that thing or person, and how I can be involved. Usually, I will communicate with that person what I'm praying for them via text, letter, or in person next time I see them. Some people don't know they have other choices until they're told. My girls might not realize they don't have to lose sleep over a test until I tell them I'm praying that they get to know God who lets them sleep in peace and safety (Psalm 4:8). We create a hopeful alternative for people when we communicate God's perspective of their situations to them. Corporate intercession, interceding with a group of people, is fantastic, and we should all do it because prayers are powerful (James 5:16). It's almost equally important to me to write down testimonies as I see answered prayers. Otherwise, I become disheartened when I don't see a prayer answered, and I start to accuse God of never doing what I ask Him to. I've found that behavior is not beneficial for our relationship. It's a lot better for us when I choose thankfulness.

Praying Scripture: Praying Scripture is a lot like singing Scripture but less melodic. I have the easiest experience with it in books like Ephesians or Colossians. I read a verse, paraphrase it into a request, and say it to God over myself or my loved ones. You can take most of the Bible and pray it over yourself. Even verses in Revelation about God as the Lamb who was slain can be taken and phrased like, "Father, reveal yourself to me as a Lamb who was slain. Show me again the significance of the sacrifice you made. Teach me your gentle nature," and so on.

Writing a Letter: Writing a letter to yourself as if it was from God is a creative method of engaging with God. I first heard of this through one of the girls I was discipling. The best way to do it, in my opinion, is to write "Dear [your name]" at the top of the page and date it, then write everything you think God would say to you if you were face to face. Fold it up, and don't look at it for at least a week. Re-read it after your set amount of time and see if anything sticks out to you. Ask the Holy Spirit to speak to you through it. God is kind and has kind things to say to you. Give yourself permission to be a part of what God is saying. A lot of times I don't need an encouraging word from someone or for someone else to pray for me, I just need to hear from God. I do myself a disservice when I live like I need someone else to hear God for me. He has made me a priest before Him (Revelation 1:5) so I have access to hear what He's saying and communicate it to others—even to myself.

Blessing Yourself: Speaking blessings over yourself is also an encouraging way to fellowship with God. I was finishing Deuteronomy and reading about Moses' blessing over Israel when the idea dawned on me. I felt inspired to write out a similar blessing for my life and read it over myself. I didn't have much to start. As I wrote, ideas flowed from my heart and out of my pen. When I felt satisfied with what I had written, I prayed it aloud over myself. I felt strengthened in my remembrance of the generosity of God. As we read the Word, we should allow space for the Holy Spirit to interact with our creativity in applying the Scripture to our lives. We don't have to simply read and reflect or read and do. We can read and live, read and act out, read and create.

Cross-Referencing: Part of my responsibility singing on worship teams at the House of Prayer was to cross-reference passages for every verse we wanted to focus on. When I was on a team focusing on Psalm 139, we would each look up three to five other verses for each verse we were singing that week. We did the same when I was on a team that was focusing on 1 Corinthians 13. After years of interacting with the Bible in that way, I now have a network of verses that cross paths and support one another racing through my mind.

Let's look at John 14:15: "If you love me, keep my commandments." That reminds me of the ten commandments, so I open Exodus 20 and start reading. Verse 6 "...but showing love to a thousand generations of those who love me and keep my commandments," stands out to me relating to John 14:15. I look back at the John reference, and I'm reminded of Matthew 22:37 when Jesus commands us to love God. Then I take a cheap shot and use Deuteronomy 6:5, which is what I remember Jesus references in the Matthew passage.

Returning to John, I think of 1 Corinthians 13 when Paul talks about doing things for God but pursuing love above all, and I add a few of those verses to my list. I can continue as long as I want and come back to add some later. All Scripture is God-breathed, which means it should all interconnect. We recognize authors, theologians, songwriters—all sorts of creative people by their quotes because many of them contain congruent messages and styles. The Bible is no different. You'll find the same themes and repeated patterns in all of it. Connecting the passages will strengthen your recollection of Scripture, and, honestly, it's a pretty fun party trick at church gatherings.

Reflecting on Relationship: I like to ask my girls which earthly relationship best represents their interactions and knowledge of God in the current season they are in. God can be Father, Friend, Bridegroom, Teacher, Brother, and so on. Sometimes, when we are more honest with ourselves, we relate to Him as a stranger, someone we used to know, an angry parent, or a distant sibling. Trying to explain our relationship with God through terms we are familiar with can help us identify what we need from God or why we are functioning the way that we do. The ways we know God will change throughout our lives. Though God remains constant, He is far above our understanding, so we will continue to learn Him for all of eternity. This exercise is good practice for me to be aware of what I'm learning about God on a given day.

In the Christian classic, Knowledge of the Holy, A. W. Tozer says, "What comes into our minds when we think about God is the most important thing about us." Our identities are heavily impacted by the way we think God relates to us. I want to reflect on what I think about God so that I don't have to miss out on who He is or who I am.

Praying through Thoughts: Movie scenes and songs get stuck in my head on the regular. I decided to start asking God and myself why certain scenes or lyrics come to mind to stay a while. I've learned so much about God and myself through moments like that. One morning, I was thinking about a scene in Avengers: End Game when Natasha and Steve are talking about the state of the world. The woman says something to the effect of, "If you came to tell me to look at the bright side, I'm going to hit you in the face with a peanut butter sandwich."

So I thought about why I thought about that scene (very meta). I realized I still had a bit of grief in me, so that's why I was reminded of that scene. I choose to be intentional throughout the day not to fake happiness or repress my sadness before God but just feel. Repressing sadness is an ineffective coping mechanism I revert to often and have to be conscious of. Conversations with God about the random thoughts in my mind make me more aware of myself, help me to be more mindful throughout my day, invite God into the small things, and take every thought captive (even the seemingly meaningless ones). It's fun for me to talk to God about things like that. If you feel like that's reading into things too much or keeping you in your head too much, let it go. There's no true benefit in constantly psycho-analyzing yourself, but becoming more self-aware is a good thing.

So many other ways of interacting with God and the Bible exist. Ask your leaders and friends what they do. Try any of the ways I've listed or come up with something on your own. If you fall more in love with God and know more of who He is (read: what you're learning about God aligns with who God says He is in the Bible) then that's good. Find what works for you, and dismiss the rest. When your season of life changes, do it again.

Podcasts, devotionals, books, small groups, and individual meetings with mentors are great, but nothing will exceed connecting with God for yourself without using a middle man. It's like switching up your spiritual diet. You get to the good stuff when you start believing that all you need to meet with God is you and God. God wants to spend time with you. It would take a twisted and broken argument of Scripture to prove otherwise. Let Him be with you, let Him speak to you, let Him love you.

Reading the Bible is a gift. The Holy Spirit is who makes it enjoyable and worthwhile. Students ask me how they can learn to hear God's voice and I love pointing them to the Bible. It's not about finishing books and memorizing Scripture (although those contribute to our faith). Life comes down to knowing God. Reading the Bible and learning to hear God's voice are one in the same. The Holy Spirit teaches us how to understand the Bible, and the Bible teaches us how to hear the Holy Spirit.

Hearing God

Reading the Bible and learning to hear God's voice are one in the same. It's like Emotional Intelligence balancing I coach people in. We all have these "soft skills" that contribute to how effectively we perceive ourselves and interact with the world. All the skills are interconnected and need to be balanced with one another in order to function well. For example, self-awareness and self-expression are two soft skills. If my self-awareness is more developed than my self-expression, I come across as melodramatic and moody because I know all the feelings inside of me but can't find a way to have them validated. If my self-expression is more developed than my self-awareness, I will be perceived as someone who overshares because I speak before I think. But when self-awareness and self-expression are balanced in their development, I can understand and communicate how I feel in a way that connects me to the people around me. Balance is key. The same principle applies to learning how to hear God's voice. We need the Holy Spirit to reveal the Bible to us, and we use the Bible to know the Holy Spirit. We learn the tone of His voice through Scriptures of His passion and gentleness. We see a well-known verse in a new light when the Holy Spirit reminds us of something related to it or highlights a word differently to us.

Some of the ways we can hear God are through a "gentle whisper," like in 1 Kings 19:11-13 or through dreams and interpretations like Daniel had. The Holy Spirit can "bear witness" to us (Romans 8:16) and help us remember things Jesus said (John 14:26). Any time I begin to feel stress overwhelm me, I feel the Spirit remind me of Scripture. I get the option to become calm again as I focus on Scriptures like "perfect love casts out all fear" or "surely I am with you." There are stranger ways God could speak to us. Writing on the wall (Daniel 5), the mouths of animals (Numbers 22), or burning bushes (Exodus 3) are perfect examples. But just because you don't have a crazy out-of-this-world encounter with the voice of God doesn't mean it's not possible.

Over and over in Ezekiel, God says, "Then you will know that I am the Lord your God." As I read through that book, I think about how God must have deeply desired to be known. He would go to great lengths to remind Israel of who He is. I think He still wants to be known. He wants to be heard. He wants to be remembered and loved. He reveals Himself to us because He loves to be known by us. He wants you to know Him intimately. It's an invitation made possible through the resurrection of Jesus. You don't have to go through anyone else anymore. You don't have to do anything but believe He's chosen to reveal Himself to you. Have faith you can hear God and trust that you have heard Him.

God will teach us to trust Him in every season. No matter what we learn about Him or what ways we grow in our knowledge of the Gospel, we always will have more reasons to trust Him. All He teaches us, all He says to us, is to build a foundation of faith in His trustworthiness. He's unlike anyone we have ever known. He will not deny His faithfulness to us. As we grow in hearing God's voice, His faithfulness can be our guide. He doesn't say anything that would discredit His promises to us. We find in Scripture that He fulfills what He speaks. All of the Word supports His faithfulness to us. We know that He won't let us down, so we can trust Him. When we see His goodness in our lives, we get to inspire others with the testimony of it.

Testimonies

Testimonies are one of my favorite displays of the Gospel. When I worked in ministry, nearly every other week we had testimony time that sometimes took up our entire two-hour staff meeting. Sure, stories can drag on or I'll get distracted. But I also heard about what God was doing which increased my faith. I keep a list of testimonies on my phone so I can check things off the list of prayer requests and add it onto my testimony list. As I was looking over my list of testimonies, I was convinced that God keeps getting better. Over the semester, I had a disciple who spent our hour-long meeting confessing her deepest insecurities and speaking truth over herself without me leading the conversation at all. That was a miracle.

I had a friend who had not been herself for months call me with restored passion for her life and a renewed sense of identity. She had been suffering from anxiety and said she felt like God wrapped her up in a blanket, covering her in peace as she was praying. Many of my friends who raise their own salaries in ministry added new financial partners to their support teams when we were praying for a steady income. I prayed for favor over one of my girls who had applied for a job she loved and the company offered it to her right after our meeting.

I've seen some of what God can do and I am in awe. He really is good. Apart from what He's done for my friends, He's good. I have numerous memories from the last few months of feeling His nearness, His kindness, His joy, and His peace. His love is like nothing else. It will make all my questions and fears disappear. I'm learning to walk in confidence that God will come through wherever He leads me. The odds are stacked in our favor because we have the favor of God as His children. I don't have to be afraid of losing things. I don't have to question what's going to happen. He's going to show up for me. When I look back over my life, I see a trail of Ebenezers all the way into the horizon as markers of His goodness following me. They serve as reminders that He is always worthy of praise.

Ascribe to the Lord

Once I was complaining to God about how I didn't feel like He was "more than enough." I barely felt like He was enough for me at all.

Let's take a quick detour here. While studying Human Development and Family Sciences in college, I took a fascinating course on Intimate Relationships. We learned about the "Four Horsemen of the Apocalypse." When you see these four issues arise in a relationship, the end is near. One of these "horsemen" is criticism, and it's antidote is actually complaining. This alters the interaction from judgment and condemnation to a communication of needs that aren't being met. The goal is to complain about the specific behavior that's not working well for the upset party rather than complaining about the partner as a person. This is not an on-going complaining relationship. Who would want to be in a relationship that consists of endless complaining? The ratio of pleasant or neutral interactions to unpleasant interactions in a healthy relationship should be about five to one. Vocalizing what is disappointing you will allow you and your loved one to work together to build a more enjoyable relationship.

I complain to God because I want to be honest with Him about how I feel like my needs aren't being met. My complaints do not come from a place of selfishness but from a desperate desire for Him and an unshakeable belief that there's more to God than I am currently experiencing. Sometimes I'm impatient for God to meet my needs. Other times, I really am just ranting from a place of selfishness. In those moments, God quickly convicts me, and we deal with that.

So, back to the beginning: I felt unsatisfied with God as I was learning about Him in the Word. I was going about my days pretty unimpressed by the amount I was seeing God do around me (which was selfish) and dissatisfied with the amount of connection I felt with God (probably had a lot to do with my selfishness this time, too). I remember sitting in the prayer chapel at work and asking God why I felt like He wasn't enough for me because I wanted Him to be everything to me. I had been waiting for God to prove Himself to me because in the moments He did, I loved it. But in the moments in between, I was judging Him (not a smart move on my part). Then I had one of those "end of Job" encounters with God. In His kindness, not with a harsh word, He rebuked me. Psalm 29:2 came to the forefront of my mind, followed by snippets of Revelation 4-5. We are to ascribe to the Lord the glory due His name. Revelation 4-5 is heaven ascribing to God the glory, honor, and praise that He deserves.

I had been ignoring the holiness of God, withholding my awe of who He is, and missing out on experiencing God in that way. He is more than enough for me—He is my everything. And even if He did nothing for me, He would still be worthy because God defines good. We cannot allow ourselves to judge God based on our perception of goodness. In God's goodness, He gives generously, and in His goodness, He revealed Himself to me.

God created us for Himself, so, of course, we will be amazed by who He is. He created us for worship. When we see Him a little bit more clearly than we have before, our natural response is to honor Him because He's always so much better than we think. I don't want to only choose worship when I am feeling God, seeing God, or feeling inspired by God. I want to worship because He was, and is, and is to come (Revelation 4:8). I want to know Him over and over in instances like the end of Job. I want to continually be humbled by his glory. That is what has been made available to us through Jesus. Worship starts with the knowledge of God.

Singing Benefits

My parents taught me to sing as an educational tool. I'm sure you can sing the abc's, and maybe, like me, you set the multiplication tables to a melody. I can recite a lot of the Prologue to

Chaucer's Canterbury Tales because my older sister had to memorize it in high school and turned it into a song. I can only read a little Spanish and form broken sentences, but I could sing multiple Spanish songs for probably half an hour without hesitation. Melodies help us remember and they make learning more fun.

I learned to sing the Word when I was young. I can't read some verses without singing the songs I learned for them in my head. I even turned some portions of Scripture into songs. I still occasionally sit down at the piano, open the Psalms, and just start singing through.

When I was growing up, worship teams I was on would pick a passage and sing the same verses week after week for two hours at a time. We called it "developing a passage," and the time paid off. The months I spent on Psalm 139 has ingrained those verses into my mind, and I love it. A lot of students ask me how to learn the Bible because they can't remember it well. I think they're hoping for something more sophisticated than making up songs.

But aside from the benefits singing the Word offers me, I think it really pleases God. Sometimes when I'm singing the Bible, I think about how He's listening to me and what He might be thinking. I think about how He knew the melodies I would choose for each phrase before my life began. I think about how long He must have been waiting for me to sing back to Him.

He's Singing Too

I am very partial to Zephaniah 3:17. When students ask me where to start meditating in their Bibles, that's where I point them to. We can learn so much about God in the density of the words. One of my favorite parts is the last line, "He rejoices over you with singing." Throughout my journals, you would find the prayer to hear God singing over me. The thought of it calms my spirit. He is a good Father.

One of my earliest memories is being in my parents room when I was five years old. My sister and I were running around dancing, and my mom was on the bed with my younger two siblings. My dad was singing and playing his guitar while he stood with one foot propped up on the bed. Much of what I know about worship stems from this memory, although I don't even remember which song we were singing. If I had to guess, it was an old worship song called "Superman." We've seen formal worship in churches. We've seen solemn worship in movies. I see offering worship to God as similar to rejoicing with my dad when I was a child.

All of God's holiness and majesty does not compete with His fatherly affection. We have as much of a right to rejoice in song with Him as we do to bow and cast our crowns at His feet. He is far above but He made Himself close. He sings over us and is overwhelmed with joy. Seeing God like that as you worship can change the whole experience.

My encouragement for worship is to stop looking around and to look around. Stop looking around because it doesn't matter how other people are worshiping or not worshiping. This is a time for you to focus on God. Worship has few rules of engagement but far too many societal expectations. Worship with child-like faith. Look around because the communities of worshipers you'll witness are beautiful. I was once worshiping on my knees with my eyes closed having what I thought was a private moment with God. I felt prompted by the Holy Spirit to open my eyes. What I saw was a memory so special it's ingrained in my memory as a mark of God's holiness. All the worship team was kneeling as they played their instruments and sang. The room was full of people humbly honoring our faithful God.

Worship isn't for judging how people praise or mimicking others behavior. It's to celebrate and commemorate the wonders of God. Approach it with a mindset of love rather than ritual or entertainment. Take in the beauty.

Thankfulness

I've hit a few depressive episodes in the last ten years. Despite my conviction to live well, I struggle for weeks at a time to enjoy life or feel motivated. During one of these episodes, I was sitting at the kitchen table in my childhood home with my dad. I confided in him about how I was feeling and he encouraged me to focus on what I was thankful for.

In all my heartbreak, loss, pain, depression, anxiety, fear, and anger, thankfulness has been a constant option. It is a weapon against the temptation to believe all is lost. A fresh perspective is sometimes all it takes to endure a troubling moment. Thankfulness can be that faithfully. Thankfulness didn't cure my depression, but it helped me acknowledge the beauty in the present world and ignited a curiosity to find more.

As I was walking out of a particularly different time in my life, I felt led by God to write out a list of one hundred things a day I was thankful for. By the fourth day, the list took only minutes to write. My conversations had shifted from focusing on the negative to testifying of the positive. I was retraining my mind to thank God always. Day by day, I felt more unexplainable joy well up inside of me. This form of worship was a pathway to finding God in everything around me. I realized I can't flee from His presence (Psalm 139:7-10), and He is the Giver of every good and perfect gift (James 1:17). Thankfulness is not a denial of the painful memories I was processing through; it was a slight pause my spirit took to recognize that not everything was terrible. I am still blessed whether I have a lot or a little.

Another time I was sitting on the back porch of my friend's house. We had both experienced being around people who valued thankfulness so strongly that we felt like we had been beaten over the head with the instruction to always be thankful. Thankfulness in all circumstances is a good thing. But in that moment it dawned on me that the Stockholm syndrome I had been experiencing with God was not a reflection of His character but a flaw in my perception of Him because of a twisted understanding of thankfulness. God does not abuse us and expect us to trust Him anyway. He does not kidnap us and require us to thank him. Our thankfulness is not meant to be an automatic response in all that happens in our lives but a product of the response to know Him better through every period of our lives.

Righteous

If you get to know me, you get to see the pretentious side of me that I wish to someday kill off entirely; she is the Hyde to my Jekyll. I compulsively correct people's grammar, obsessively point out typos, and sarcastically tease friends for their mistakes. My friend Meredith had a habit of saying "whole nother" instead of "whole other" when she was speaking and I would religiously whisper "other" as she continued in her stories. In my mind, I was Jim Halpert staring at the cameras in The Office. In reality, I was obnoxious. She says "whole nother" to this day, but now it's purely to frustrate me for her own entertainment.

As I learn to let go of my self-righteousness and pride, I am careful not to pendulum swing toward careless and reckless living. Working toward that sweet spot of righteousness has led me to discoveries and victories. Discoveries have taught me the purpose of doing what is right; victories have occurred in overcoming what had kept me from doing what was right. I don't want to live like I'm better than everyone else but I also don't want to live in a way in which others are living better than me.

We all live our best lives when we live and love like Jesus. Jesus said if we love Him, we will follow His commands (John 15). So if obedience is related to abiding in love, I want to do what is right in the eyes of Love. I am learning both how to obey and how to love. They go hand in hand. In living righteously, I increase my capacity to give and receive love. I have a lot to learn, but I'm seeing that the benefits are worth the effort.

Legalism

I hear Christians, cautious to avoid becoming like the Pharisees, talk about other Christians who are "religious" as opposed to their counterparts who are "free from legalism." I don't want to be like the Pharisees Jesus so boldly reprimanded. But I've come to a realization that we don't have to live in fear of legalism. We simply have to love Jesus. Nothing is religious if God is the center of your attention. When we fear legalism, we have a tendency to shy away from spiritual disciplines. Fasting, prayer, reading the word, and attending Church are all good things that can easily become legalistic, or they could be vessels through which we experience more of God. We need a perspective shift, not to abandon ship.

This is where we need to start snacking on the fruit of the Spirit called self control. I've told my girls I'd rather have the self control of the Spirit keeping me from sin than have to cut off my right hand. If cutting off my hand were what it takes then absolutely I would. But we have the Spirit to teach us not to sin and how to control our thoughts and actions. Legalism is just another form of sin; it's idolizing the religion of Christianity over Christ. Living in the Spirit keeps us from this idolatry. His holiness can capture my attention and permeate any hyper-spiritual ritual or old tradition I am participating in. We don't have to be afraid of being "too righteous." Righteousness is following the Spirit, and He will lead us into all truth. Keep your eyes on Him, and you can't miss that path.

We were meant to be holy. Holiness has less to do with right and wrong and more to do with depending on God or not. The Pharisees knew the law, but they depended on the law rather than God. The disciples missed the mark so many times, but they depended on Jesus. When they struggled to cast out a demon, Jesus told them they needed to increase their faith through fasting and prayer. His guidance implied that they needed to cultivate a lifestyle of dependence on God, not a "how-to" instruction manual on casting out demons. Most of the apparent "how-to's" of the Bbile are actually practicals of dependence on God rather than directions to produce intended results. I've had interactions with leaders of the faith who seem like they care more about being right rather than loving. It's neither encouraging nor inspiring. Sometimes my desire to be right exceeds my pursuit of holiness. Pride gets in the way and trips me up. I can trust that God will oppose the pride in me and teach me in His mercy.

Teachers of the law and Pharisees were watching when Jesus told the parable of the Prodigal Son to a group of tax collectors and sinners. The father's comment to the older son in the story was likely a shared sentiment of the Father toward the teachers of the law and Pharisees. He said, "You have always been with me, and everything I have is yours. But we had to celebrate and be glad because this brother of yours was dead and is alive again; he was lost and is found" (Luke 15:31-32).

God loves our faithfulness but He's not holding us to a standard of unattainable perfection. He became our righteousness (2 Corinthians 5:21). We don't stand a chance without Him. Being knowledgeable is a wonderful and helpful thing but it's not everything. When we let pride and self-righteousness get in the way of relationship, we miss out on celebrating with God.

Blake, who I mentioned earlier, once said, "I just had to be willing to get it wrong, so I could have the opportunity to get it right." Give yourself the freedom to get it wrong and to fail. I don't mean you should be inconsiderate of your relationship with God; I mean you should try without fear of failure and fear of disappointing God. If you're embracing your identity as a child of God, you've got it right. Everything else can be messy if it happens to be messy. Jesus is so good at making things clean. Run to the Father, and you'll find the narrow path of righteousness underneath your feet.

Freedom of Righteousness

Doing what is right produces personal freedom. You know when you tell a little lie, and then you have to live on guard to conceal it? That's such a burden. Living righteously offers the same lightness as living honestly. I've counted the cost of following God (more times than I care to admit), but it is always worth it to me. Or I have someone wiser than me remind me that it's worth it. Don't let anything stand in your way of that freedom. You may be struggling with something right now or did something wrong. It likely just crossed your mind. Confess that sin today, and walk in freedom.

Righteousness is the road we're invited to travel on now. We aren't alone in a dark forest wandering. God is taking us step by step toward what is right. Just follow Him. One of my favorite prayers to pray is for God to expose what I need to let go of.

Sometimes it's sin, sometimes it's lies, sometimes it's doubt. Getting rid of things that are keeping you from righteousness is like a productive spring cleaning. Don't let shame keep you from organizing that closet. It feels so good to know and see yourself as righteous by the grace of God.

Doing what is right may be less or more difficult than the alternatives. The level of difficulty is not the sole indicator of what you should do. For Jesus in the garden of Gethsemane, going to the cross was literally hellish. But He was moved with compassion for the hurting people around Him. I imagine the insight that His sacrifice would save and heal multitudes was the joy set before Him. In our zeal for God, we may be tempted to take the more challenging path in order to follow God. But, while God does lead us into the wilderness, He also leads us by quiet streams in green pastures. The best way to know what to do is to ask Him. Then go where He guides you. Obedience will always reap the peaceful fruits of righteousness.

Good Fruit

When we do what is right, we produce good fruit in our lives. This is the truth of sowing and reaping. Godly and upright living isn't just for the sake of doing what is right, although if it were, that would be enough. God has designed the nature of the world to harvest the fruit of the work we set our hands to. Part of realizing we have power in Christ is realizing our choices have consequences. As we pursue holiness and choose righteousness, we are rewarded with knowing God and experiencing His nearness. Likewise, if we pursue wickedness and choose disobedience, we experience disconnection from God and feel far from Him.

If I follow God in what He has called me to, I'll feel an underlying sense of purpose and lead others into more of God. We naturally produce the fruit of the Spirit when we live according to the Spirit, just like we naturally imitate the characteristics of friends we spend the most time with. We can see our hearts through the fruit we produce. Good fruit looks like love, joy, peace, patience, kindness, goodness, gentleness, faithfulness, and self-control (Galatians 5:22-23).

Letting God prune us is a humbling, necessary, and redemptive process. I think we often taint our witnesses as Christians because we are too proud or too afraid to let God prune us. We settle for producing some good fruit while the rest is unripe or rotting. God is gentle in His correction and He disciplines out of love. Asking Him to expose our shortcomings or sin and replace everything with better fruit is asking for blessing. We will be healthier and happier when we allow God to uproot dying foundations.

I challenge you not to make excuses for yourself. If you notice bad fruit in your life or someone calls it out in you, take it before God and let Him redeem you. He's not trying to make you perfect because He's ashamed of your bad fruit. He wants to make you holy because He has a purpose for your life unto His glory. Remember, His love is not self-serving and His glory glorifies us as well because of His incredible grace. As we live lives that are pleasing to Him, we get to live in the love and favor of the Lord Almighty. His grace provides for us and His peace protects us. He works all things together for our good and restores all that is stolen. As we experience His glory, we become more like Him. As the Gardener, He wants to help you produce good fruit.

Honor Your Mom and Dad

Jesus was not shy when He quoted part of the Ten Commandments saying, "Honor your father and mother" and "anyone who curses their father or mother will be put to death" in Matthew 15. No parent is perfect and all make mistakes. I've heard too many disturbing stories of how poorly parents have treated their offspring. Their children would find it easy to dishonor them and some might even feel cause to curse them. But God enlightened us to the secret of living a long and full life: to honor our fathers and mothers.

Forgiving your parents for the ways they failed is one of the best gifts you can give to yourself. A lot of our parents had good intentions that just didn't come across well in action. As we mature, we need to learn to change our perspective toward our parents' words and actions. Think about what they said and what they really meant. Think about what they did and why they probably did things that way. Hold onto the intentions behind it all, and let go of the rest. We don't have to keep them indebted to us, regardless of what kinds of parents they were (or still are).

As I mentioned earlier, my parents would have us respond to their requests with "immediately, completely, and without complaining" when we were kids. We were taught to be obedient in this manner. At some point, their wise advice turned into a robotic response for me and my siblings. Their instruction taught me how to be prompt, effective, and cheerful in serving, but, eventually, it also led to me becoming half-hearted and resentful in my serving. Upon this realization, I could have spent the rest of my life feeling like they owed me as parents for creating this mindset. But I could also recognize my responsibility in receiving and processing the information they gave me. At any point, I could have chosen self-awareness to prevent that robotic effect and I didn't. Now, I can choose to reverse the robotic effect by acknowledging what the intent was behind their instruction and releasing the learned habit of mindlessly obeying.

I don't want to dishonor my parents because they are real and beautiful human beings. Before they were ever my parents, they were loved by God. For whatever reasons, He chose them to bring me into the world. It's their DNA that produced mine and their blood in my veins. Their victories and their shortcomings, their propensities and their talents, are all parts of what made me who I am. Honoring them is easy because it's not based on their character and actions; my honor towards them is based on how God sees them. We have to learn to see the generations above us with respect and gratefulness.

In Daniel 5, King Belshazzar was killed because he ignored the work of God in his predecessor's life. King Nebuchadnezzar had a crazy reign marked by pride and being humbled by God. If King Belshazzar had learned from history, he may have lived a different life. But by ignoring it all, he was destroyed. We are given answers and truth in learning the history of those before us. Our parents' stories hold keys to our futures. For the same reason we honor the history of a nation, we should honor our parents' roles in our lives. If nothing else, they hold wisdom in their experiences.

In honoring our parents, we honor God. He can teach you how to honor them when they have lived less-than-honorable lives. He can give you wisdom through what you know about them if you don't know them well. He can restore relationships where they need to be restored and heal what has been hurt. Our responsibility is to be honoring however we can be.

Honoring does not always mean obeying. In many of our lives, we will face conflict with our parents. Individuating from our families of origin, we may disagree with our parents or feel led by God in a different direction. God is our Father and we are His children. These are our primary identities in Christ. The New Living Translation of Luke 14 says, "If you want to be my disciple, you must, by comparison, hate everyone else—your father and mother, wife and children, brothers and sisters—yes, even your own life."

What God is leading you into trumps everything else in your life. But what God is leading you into should not be mutually exclusive with honoring your parents to some degree because that is what God wants for you. We have to remember that what God leads us into will not conflict with what God values. God is a family man. You may defy your parents wishes for your life. You may argue with them. You may never share a perspective on something. But if God is leading you into something, you need to follow that, and you need to find a way to honor your parents through it all. Your relationship doesn't have to end because you disagree.

Your parents can be great spiritual leaders, but they are not the sole spiritual authorities of your life. As a believer, you have the Holy Spirit in you. God made a way so that no one would need someone else come before Him on their behalf. You get to talk to God, you get to hear God, you get to respond to God. There is wisdom in a multitude of counselors so ask your parents' advice. Ask other spiritual leaders for feedback. Get a mentor and submit to a church, but don't surrender your right to hear God for yourself. He has given Himself to you. You get to learn from Him the balance between trusting what you think He's saying to you and following what your leaders are suggesting to you. Righteousness goes deeper than our action; it goes all the way to the state of our hearts.

Motivation

During my senior year of college, I was taught how to distinguish motivation from ability. We cannot do some things because we simply cannot do them. Other things we cannot do because we do not want to do them, but we don't always acknowledge that's the reason. When I find myself faced with a task that I don't want to attempt, I ask myself how much money it would take to get me to do it. If there is an amount, no matter how ridiculous, then I know my core problem is motivation, not ability. For all the money in the world, I could not write a dissertation in a day. I couldn't be an Olympic athlete or an astronaut. For free, I would meet up with someone and discuss life. For a hundred dollars, I would coach a student in emotional intelligence. For a thousand dollars, I might try my hand at plumbing. Learning the difference between motivation and ability can help us identify the barriers holding us back from doing what is right.

Patient endurance is a lost quality for many, largely due to the quest for immediate gratification. We aren't aware enough to differentiate between lack in motivation and lack of ability, so we give up altogether. I remember being reduced to a confused pair of eyes in a sea of blank expressions when my high school American Literature teacher lectured us on the importance of grit. My classmates and I were so unfamiliar with the notion of work ethic and at a loss for why courageous resolve was of such high value.

Academically, I was lacking grit. Later I recognized that, religiously, grit made so much sense to me. I learned to bridge the gap from motivation in spirituality to motivation in other areas of my life. We know perseverance produces good things but that isn't always the most compelling factor for working hard. In developing perseverance, I remember to align my heart with what God says is good for me. I persevere because the kindest Being to ever exist tells me it's good for me to (Romans 5:3-5).

This is the fuel for my integrity. I do things I don't want to do because I love God. He puts me in positions of influence that require some things I don't enjoy. I want to honor Him by honoring every aspect of the load He has given me. Working hard produces longer lasting effects. Quick fixes often fall apart just as quickly. Grit motivates me because hard, long work produces better results. It's saving time and energy in the long run. Shortcuts won't produce results like intentional labor will so eventually we'll have to redo what we've already done. But when we put in the effort on the front end, we can reap the rewards for a long time.

Probably my greatest annoyance in personal development is pendulum swinging instead of slow and steady work. I watch people set a goal for themselves and, in their excitement, they go to the extreme but never settle into a healthy medium. For example, someone spends too much of their day on social media. Instead of learning to use their time well through self-control, they delete the app altogether. A week, a month, a year later they give social media another chance and find themselves enchanted by the same mind-numbing scrolling all over again. Pendulum swings are short-cuts with short-term results. Take the scenic route in achieving personal development to produce long-term benefits. We're not in a hurry.

Living righteously requires the development of motivation. We have the ability to do what is right through the grace of God but our lack of motivation can keep us from choosing a righteous life. A lack of patient endurance, a craving for immediate gratification, or a rush for progress will send us on paths we don't want to be on. Righteousness is a road we are intended to walk down, not run back and forth across. Align your drive to be righteous with perseverance and you'll feel more secure in your steps. We have to pair our desires with actions, our faith with works. They compliment each other well.

Self-control is one of my favorite fruits of the Spirit, but it sounds less appealing than love or joy. The value I see in self-control is the freedom of knowing my limits. I often use the example of children on a playground when I explain this concept to the girls I disciple. I learned in college that children behave differently on playgrounds depending on whether or not a fence is present. Without a fence, children are much more likely to stick to the center of the playground. With a fence, children will play on the playset and explore further out around the allotted space. Self-control is our personal playground fence. It creates the boundary for us to safely play and explore in the world. The Holy Spirit grows this fruit inside of us when we abide in the love of Jesus (John 15). Finding the motivation to do what is right doesn't have to look like hitting yourself over the head with a book. It looks like getting to know the Holy Spirit more intimately and letting Him show you how to live. As you learn how to live, you have to learn how to communicate your expectations and boundaries to others.

Healthy Confrontation

Confrontation is sometimes required to do what is right. Conflict is rarely anyone's cup of tea and confrontation can be a stress-inducing activity. So take a deep breath and relax. No one has to confront anyone at this moment. I want to equip you to handle future conflicts with effectiveness and ease. Let's begin!

Identify the Issue: Emotions can make us feel like problems are much bigger than they actually are. You'll want to take a moment and identify the root of the issue.. Acknowledge the impact of the core point of disconnection but also discern the difference between the root and its fruits. Ask "why" and keep asking. Dig through deeper issues of the problem until you reach the root. Before initiating the confrontation, simplify the issue into one simple sentence. Then begin identifying your expectations for future involvement.

Identify the Relationship: Imagine you and the person you're at odds with share a bank account. Every interaction you have adds to or withdraws from your relational account. If you're planning on initiating a confrontation, you need to have enough money saved up in the bank to use because conflict is expensive relationally. Saving up money looks like engaging in neutral or positive interactions. Also, determining what you want from the relationship is necessary. If your relationship is ending, it's probably not worth confronting issues and your energy would be better spent learning to peacefully let go.

Create a Safe Space: Confrontation doesn't have to feel threatening for anyone involved. Ask if you can set up a time to meet, do it in a private space if appropriate, and breathe. Anyone with social skills can read body language. They'll pick up on nervousness, so stay calm. Although it may be a tense situation, nobody is in physical danger; confrontation shouldn't happen alone and face to face if there is a risk of physical endangerment. Creating a safe space also might involve remembering why a conversation is worth having. The more confident I feel in what I believe, the easier it is for me to hear what the other person thinks and find common ground.

Reconnect: Assertiveness is often associated with disconnection. But effective assertiveness actually builds connection—it doesn't break it. When confronting someone, the primary goal should be reconnection. Find a common goal to work toward and use honesty to make progress. Practically, this looks like thanking the person for meeting with you, stating your single-sentence summary of the problem, and giving them space to reject or accept what you shared. Rejection is a risk of confrontation, but developing deeper, more fulfilling relationships is usually worth the risk. If the other person accepts your initial overview of the issue, begin working through the problem and discussing expectations for moving forward. Let them know you appreciate their willingness to have the conversation you just engaged in.

Confrontation creates space for healthy boundaries so we can be the best versions of ourselves and respect the best versions of the people in our lives. We confront one another to unify, to communicate what ways we have been triggered (by disappointment, exhaustion, anger, or other unpleasant emotions), and to interact in ways that produce positive emotions in both people involved.

It's good to keep in mind that if you're hurt, the other person is probably hurt as well. At the very least, the other person may be defensive. Their pain does not invalidate yours; you can both be hurting. Let down your defenses and communicate in an honest yet gentle way.

When coaching clients in Emotional Intelligence on assertiveness or emotional expression, I remind them to celebrate when they assert or express themselves. If it's hard for you to speak up, whether you achieve the intended results or not, you should acknowledge the bravery it took. The effort was not wasted, regardless of the outcome. If people try to confront someone and decide not to ever again because it didn't turn out how they wanted, then all of their relationships will suffer because one did. Don't let one poor outcome cost you the quality of future relationships. Be brave and try again. That's the only way to get stronger.

Growing up, I was horrified by conflict. Confrontation was the bane of my existence and I was told repeatedly to learn how to assert myself. As I've grown, I've been able to see how mutually beneficial confrontation is. Conflict is inevitable, but it's not as difficult as we give it credit for. Don't see it as the monster in the closet or the beast you have to slay. It's not an excuse to be aggressive and shouldn't be constant (remember the relational bank). Call it what it is: a tool for stronger, healthier connections.

Loving God

I hope you've been able to catch a glance of the immeasurable greatness God has made available to you. The Father wants to be known by you and Jesus is the Way. He sustains your hunger for righteousness and fills you with good things. Say yes to Him. Abundant life flows from Him and He has more to give to you.

As you receive His love, you'll want to make room in your heart for more. Loving yourself in a godly way will help create that space. Let's address hurt, limitations, and exhaustion to open up the windows of your soul and let the light in.

Part II: Loving You

"As the Father has loved Me, so I have loved you. Now remain in My love." John 15:9

Hopeful

Let me be honest with you about a life-long battle I had with hope that culminated in a five-month stint of disappointment. Hope was the anchor that dragged my soul to the bottom of the ocean to drown. I had dreams—good dreams—for myself and others that were dashed to pieces. I wanted to see the people I loved overcome cancer. I wanted strong, vibrant relationships. I wanted everything that is possible according to the Word to happen with a just word from my mouth—prosperity, miracles, perfect gifts.

I wouldn't have known my hope was in my circumstances and not in God until what I wanted fell out of reach. I wouldn't have said it aloud, but I thought I was kinder than God—more faithful, more passionate, more caring. I thought I was hopeless; I was wrong. I was entitled and proud, which is nothing like the love of God. His love is not self-seeking or prideful; His love always perseveres (1 Corinthians 13).

A gentle conviction graciously and eventually led me to see what I thought was hopelessness was bitterness and hurt masquerading in self-righteousness and powerlessness. I am still in danger of falling into the same mistake of supposed hopelessness again because hope is as mysterious to me as love and faith. But I found a treasure in the midst of my pain—a glimpse of real hope. Hopelessness is a choice; it is not a result forced upon us because Hope is always an option.

Heavy Hope
I sat in a sermon during my spring break in California, and

tears rolled down my cheeks. For years, hope had been an elusive and beautiful concept that I eagerly pursued. If you could walk into my mind and open the door marked "hope," you'd find it fully furnished with experiences that turned out in my favor, verses about not being shaken, and song lyrics that I repeated to myself melodramatically in hard times until I got my breakthrough. I love that God is hopeful and that, of all things, hope is one of the three that remain forever. Throughout all of eternity we will have better and better to look forward to. I love that God is the kind of leader who puts a door of hope in the valley of trouble (Hosea 2). He makes another way, gives another option, and provides good opportunities in the driest seasons.

But as I sat in a message on hope that day, hope was heavy—an experience I was more familiar with than I preferred. The speaker declared in amusement and authority the lies we often believe that make us feel hopeless. "I have no value. I have no future. I am unwanted..." I could understand the humor because I was familiar with his style of teaching and I have overcome lies in my life as well that are now nothing more than a joke to me. A year ago it would have been difficult to refute the idea that I am not enough, but after taking thoughts captive long enough, it doesn't have much power over me. These tears falling down were silent and from a different place.

Years ago, my grandma was diagnosed with Parkinson's Disease, which only advanced as she aged and grew in frustration at the incapabilities of her own body. Only a few weeks before, I learned my grandpa was about to start chemotherapy. He was so upset about it that he didn't speak to me for a few weeks, which was highly unusual for our relationship.

I asked God what I had to be hopeful for in the midst of these situations. Hope that I would see them again in eternity did not make much sense when it came to interacting with them. I didn't feel like it was kind to tell them everything would be okay because they'd eventually die but we will reunite when I die as well. Hope that they'd be completely healed didn't seem to feel right either, not because I believed God was incapable or unwilling, but because they had lived very long lives and would eventually die like all of us. I didn't feel led to tell them they'd be healed while they were trying to muster the strength to make it through the day.

That's when I felt God share with me a piece of hope for

57

their situations. I could hope that despite all the pain and frustration, their later-lives could still be full of life and love. When I spoke with them or visited them, I could walk into the room and offer a new perspective of hope—that their lives have value, and they are wanted. This gave me the freedom to rejoice when rejoiced, mourn when they mourned, and still be a life-giving source for them. This hope fueled my patience when my grandmother couldn't finish a sentence, and hope pushed me toward deeper care instead of worry when my grandfather stumbled as he walked. Recalling this hope was my pathway to peace when I would get off the phone with them and feel so heartbroken that I could cry. Hope combated my deepest fears and became a doorway through which I obtained power, love, and a sound mind.

His yoke is easy, and his burden is light (Matthew 11:30). He trades sorrow for joy (Psalm 30:11). We will not be put to shame (Isaiah 40:31). He leads us by streams of water and restores our soul (Psalm 23:3). Hope deferred makes the heart sick, but a longing fulfilled is a tree of life (Proverbs 13:12). Don't let hope go. Dream about your life with God. Hope will usher you into greatness.

Hope and Grief

A few weeks later I was in a prayer meeting trying to process the news that my grandfather's cancer had progressed to stage four and was in his bloodstream. I knew the worst thing I could have done for myself was put the "bandaid" of hope over this gaping wound and try to move forward. I asked God to lead me in hope as I dealt with the pain. In response, I felt Him inspire me with guidelines for coping and grieving:

Feel pain.

Don't focus too much on what I am not doing that you miss what I am.

Shut up the inner theologian, and sit with Me.

Acknowledge My nearness is your good; I am near to the brokenhearted (Psalm 34:18).

When you feel My Spirit move in you, move.

Feeling pain is difficult. Sometimes we don't need just prayer, we need affection and community. Be honest with yourself about your needs, and be honest with your people. Just say you're struggling instead of labeling it something holier than it needs to be. Let people love you—maybe through prayer, maybe through listening, maybe through a combination of things.

Be honest in your grief. I've written things to God in my journal that I knew weren't true. But in expressing all the junk within me, I made room for the Holy Spirit to fill me. Here's an excerpt of what I wrote when I was struggling with my grandpa's sickness:

> "I don't understand what I'm supposed to do. I've been given authority but it looks like it's not working. I've been given freedom and it looks like I'm not giving it away. My hope is heavy and I'm afraid. I don't know whether to ask for healing or command it, to pursue restoration of his body or his relationship with Jesus. Both are more than I can handle. I feel like I'm selfish but I know you desire life. I don't know how to separate my desires from your perfect will. I don't know how to grieve and feel while pushing for better. I don't know how to let you hold me when I feel like you're betraying me. Please intervene. I don't want it to be alright. I want it to be right. I want things my way. He's mine. He's yours." — June 30, 2019

God doesn't deserve to be spoken to the way I've spoken to Him at times. He is holy and righteous. He is King. But He has given me a relationship with Him through Christ in which I am His child. This relationship is better than even the best father-child relationship we've witnessed on earth. But His grace does not enable me to blaspheme His character—that's not the point. His grace allows me to express my offense in pursuit of a better relationship with Him.

We get nowhere in relationships being resentful or fake and invalidating our feelings. In all of my anger toward God that I've expressed, I've found freedom, nearness, and a deeper love for who He is. That's the point of grace. Get real with your grief. Don't cover it up before God. He knows something is wrong. Let

Him in.

The writer of Psalm 42 expressed his pain before God in deeply emotive language. He held little to nothing back as he processed his grief. Look at some of the content that is a part of our Holy Book:

> "My tears have been my food day and night, while people say to me all day long, 'Where is your God?'...Why, my soul, are you downcast? Why are you so disturbed within me?...My soul is downcast within me; therefore I will remember you...Deep calls unto deep in the roar of your waterfalls; all your waves and breakers have swept over me...I say to God my Rock, 'Why have you forgotten me? Why must I go about mourning, oppressed by the enemy? My bones suffer in mortal agony as my foes taunt me, saying to me all day long, 'Where is your God?'"

These sentiments appear far out of alignment with rejoicing in the Lord always (Philippians 4:4). But it's in the release of his pain that he makes room for God later on in the chapter, saying, "Put your hope in God, for I will yet praise him, my Savior and my God... therefore I will remember you...By day the Lord directs his love and at night his song is with me, a prayer to the God of my life." Expressing hurt does not inherently cause division. Confrontation, when used correctly, is meant for the restoration of relationships. You are the Bride of Christ. You are a child of the King. In confidence of your God-ordained identity, like Esther, approach the throne. There is no condemnation in Christ. He can take your brokenness and make it beautiful. Release the pressure of trying to bring Him something beautiful from your brokenness. He is the Redeemer, not you. Give Him a chance to strengthen your relationship with Him. He won't turn you away.

I met with Bob Beckwith, the director of the UGA Wesley Foundation, after my grandfather passed away. I was struggling to make it out of bed each morning and to be present throughout my day. All I knew to do was keep showing up and expect that one day things would be different. I was eating as much as I could with no appetite, laying down for bed each night without sleep, and driving into work each day without anything to offer.

Bob was kind enough to sit with me while I cried and he listened to me.

In response he said, "You're grieving, but you're not fragile. You're hurting, but you're strong." In all the brokenness that accompanies loss, I had lost perspective. Strength does not always look like thriving; sometimes strength is just standing up. Grief does not discount us from our battles; grief is another battlefield. Day by day, we trust that God will bring us victory as we follow Him.

My grief didn't hinder me from discipling my girls. Some of the best conversations we had that semester were in those desperately difficult days. I would run to the prayer chapel between meetings and beg God to fill our time together because I had nothing to give. Then I got to watch Him come through for them and for me. My grief didn't stop me from connecting with my family. They cared for me so well when I was falling apart. I never expected so much grace from them. My grief didn't remove me from the presence of God. He was as near as He always is and comforting and loving me well. My grief was self-preservation; it was the natural response to the devastation I was experiencing. Through my grief I found moments of peace and restoration. In my grief, God spoke strength into my identity as He brought me healing.

Desperate Hope

Months after my grandfather's death, I spontaneously decided to attend my home church. The speaker was someone who joined the church long after I had left. Toward the end of his message, he asked, "How desperate are you to live?" I could feel my spirit jump at those words. All it takes to keep going is a desperation to live. He reminded us that this life is a war; we do what we have to do to survive until we get our breakthrough.

For months I had been feeling desperation, which led me to fully depend on God to help me to the next step. Desperation is a gift as we wait for breakthrough. The desire to live is a blessing, sustaining our hope. Life is part of the joy set before us as we endure pain because life is part of the inheritance we received in Christ.

I learned in those months just how much it bothers me when people say they cannot do something. "I can't do this." "There's no way." "I could never do that." We can do anything (Philippians 4:13); we just don't give up. Perseverance is a part of the hope process. You'll be amazed at what you're capable of when you determine to patiently work toward what you want.

Four months after my grandpa passed away, another family member was diagnosed with stage three cancer. The news triggered memories of all the people in my life who have gone through or passed away from cancer. I noticed fear enter my mind and I was enticed. But I felt the Holy Spirit whisper in my spirit, "Cancer is not a death sentence." Hope means I don't let my past experiences determine my future, I let God. It will be difficult to believe all over again that cancer is not the end, but hope is the better alternative to accepting defeat. Hope will make me stronger. Hope will see miracles in one way or another.

Hope and Silence

I've heard lots of students talk about how God doesn't answer prayers even though they want to believe He does. They talk about the disappointments they've experienced or how they've been asking for something for so long, and He still won't give it to them. I've counseled many students as they press for God's direction about their futures. I've stood alongside students as they've literally cried out to see healing only to learn how to cope with death or sickness in the end.

I've been considering the silence of God. My dad brought it up in conversation over text after I had been dwelling on the idea for a week. God was silent in between Malachi and Matthew during what's known as the "400 Years of Silence." Isaiah describes the Crucifixion and implies Jesus' silence as He was being led to the Cross like a lamb led to the slaughter. Then in Revelation, we are told there was silence in heaven for half an hour in the writer's vision.

In our conversation, my dad said, "Sometimes God uses silence to communicate with you more effectively than words ever could." God is not spiteful. He doesn't stonewall us or give us the silent treatment as a power play. This would be in opposition to His kindness and faithfulness. Dad believes that God uses His silence as a relational tool to increase intimacy.

He continued, "Imagine someone starts to believe that they don't really need God. Then, instead of hearing His voice when they are facing difficult decisions, He remains silent so they can perceive their need for Him. Job is a perfect example. He never would have believed he was leaning on his own righteousness until the enemy attacked, then his friends attacked, and in the midst of it, God was silent for a season. Then Job begins to declare his own righteousness and accuse God." God speaks after that season of silence.

The Shulamite ignores her beloved's knock on the door in the book of Song of Solomon, so he leaves. She is alone in a season of seeking after him before she is reunited with him. This is a metaphor for times when we don't respond to God in the moment of opportunity He gives us and we miss out on deepening our intimacy with Him. The chapter represents seasons of our lives that are usually marked by loneliness and feeling like God is far away. But, as we know from the promise of Matthew 28:20 and the rest of Song of Solomon, God is always with us.

The silence of God appears again when the disciples are on a boat in a storm with Jesus and He's sleeping. He is quiet, but He is not distant. He always responds in time, whether His response is what you expected or something different. The beautiful thing about this story is that the disciples woke Jesus up (Mark 4). Their relationships with Him and connection to Him gave them access to ask for Him to respond in a time that He was silent.

In considering my own history with God, I have been mulling over the prayers God hasn't answered. After much thought, I've realized there has not been a single one. Circumstances certainly haven't always turned out like I asked God for them to, but I haven't experienced a time when God did not respond to me. To my credit, I am relentlessly persistent. I push until I get my answer. But it works.

I've learned to let go of expectations and hold onto the conversation I have in relationship with God. My prayers must be in line with what God wants, otherwise there is no point. So when I don't get my way, I try to determine if it was God's will or mine. If it was God's will for things to turn out differently than I asked, I pray that I'll understand or not be offended. If it was my will, I know what God has is better than what I can ask for. Regardless of the turnout of any prayer, the conversation with God continues because He always shows up when I choose to show up.

When God doesn't do what we ask Him to do, it's not because He doesn't answer our prayers. Prayer is the conversation you're having with Him, not the magic trick by which we get what we want. One of the fundamental truths we cannot lose sight of is that God speaks. Don't be held back by the lie that God is distant. Elijah taunts the prophets of Baal at Mount Carmel because their god isn't responding to their requests. He jokes about Baal being occupied or unable to hear. He is unwaveringly confident that our God is not distant, He's not too busy, and He doesn't ignore us.

God does not ignore you. If you are not convinced that God is near to you, find the truth in Scripture. It's there. Sometimes it's hard to live out what we believe, but try anyway. God will answer you. Let Him say what He wants to say. Don't ignore Him or give up in impatience. Choose love when you don't feel it and watch a miracle happen. If you draw near to God, He will draw near to you.

Dorrie Garner, an evangelist in Athens, was sharing her testimony at a service. At some point in her life she had asked God for something big that she never received from Him. She really wanted it and had really prayed for it, but she didn't get it. As she wrapped up her testimony for us, she said, "I don't believe God left that prayer unanswered, I believe He said no. He said no to my prayer, but He said yes to me." In not getting what she asked for, she found herself in a life wilder than her dreams. She was not rejected by God; she was accepted by Him and given more than she bargained for.

This is the God I know: the One who is so loving that even when He says no, He chooses us. Knowing the truth about God will change the way we pursue hope. Aligning our hearts with truth helps us see through the rejection we feel to the kindness of His wisdom. God has things to say to us, and in time we will understand. Hear Him.

Just because He doesn't speak doesn't mean He doesn't answer prayer. At times I've been angry with God, I think I would have been skeptical of anything He said. I'd be too defensive to hear the heart behind His words. In a world where we only know in part, that could be dangerous. Sometimes sensing His presence is just as comforting as hearing His voice.

I was at lunch with a close friend who had been unstable in her mental health. She sat across from me talking so fast I could hardly keep up, only to break down crying right in front of me at the table in the back of the restaurant. I wanted to tell her that I love her. I wanted to tell her she was going to be okay, and I could lead her to resources that could help her, that she was never meant to feel so insecure, lost, and broken. But my friend was so defensive. I could feel impending rejection for anything I might say before I even opened my mouth. So I didn't say a word. But my silence was screaming, "I love you. I believe you in you. You are safe. I have hope for you."

Before I could say anything, my friend got up and left. I cried the whole way home, despite knowing she needed space and wanting to honor that for her. In all of my silence, my spirit was interceding that she could get to a stable place to receive my love and let down her walls to let me in. Love is patient and not self-seeking. It is not forceful. So I chose to believe in hope and faith and love that God would bring her peace and bring us back together. He did.

I believe God does the same for me. In my fear and confusion, He respects my struggle. He gives me the space I ask for when I build up walls around my heart. But in the silence, He is screaming His faithful love over me.

Matthew 15 tells the story of a desperate mother crying out on behalf of her suffering daughter. Jesus doesn't answer her at first, then he rejects her. But as she persists, He responds. He celebrates her faith and grants her request.

You can push. You can continue crying out when God is silent and maybe even at times when He says no. Remember the message God has screamed from heaven since the beginning of time: He loves you. Every time He is silent, we have to know love is the source and the vessel and the end destination.

Disappointment

Don't guard yourself from disappointment when you pray. We can't align our prayers with our perspectives of realities; we need to align them with the hope of God's reality. Dreading disappointment doesn't make dealing with disappointment any easier. Someone challenged me and a group of others to write something big we were believing God for on a piece of paper. It was hard to write down that I wanted to see my grandfather get healed. It was harder to see grandfather losing strength and to keep praying. It was even harder to find that piece of paper in my purse after he had passed away two weeks later. However, it was not hard to let God comfort me, to allow Him space to sit in my pain with me, and to fill me with hope in Him because I hadn't been preparing myself for inevitable disappointment. I was sowing into my relationship with God through prayer.

Confirmation bias is when we believe something will happen so it ends up happening. It's also called a self-fulfilling prophecy. When we pray with limitations on God, already expecting Him not to come through on some level, we break our trust with God when we don't see the miracle. We mistrust, not because God deserves mistrust but because we were believing He was never as good as He says He is and gave ourselves evidence to build a case against Him. We can have all the love for God in the world, but if we don't have hope and faith, it's a relationship that can't be sustained.

Tell Him when it hurts. Tell Him when you're disappointed. God isn't angry at your anger or bitter at your bitterness. He does not require an eye for an eye. His love is really big enough to cover the multitudes of sin we feel. My boss encouraged me to take time off work one week when I was really struggling to function because of my grief. I went to the International House of Prayer Atlanta for the rest of the day and the entire following day to get real with God. I had to fight off shame as I wrote out the depths of anger that I felt toward God in my journal. I knew it was breaking God's heart that I would say those things, but it would break His heart more for me to disconnect from Him to spare His feelings.

He doesn't ask us to hide from Him. He's with us in the mess. I turned off my theological filter and wrote some of the most heretical things I've ever expressed, and I knew I was mis-understanding God. But I felt strongly that I needed to be honest in order to let Him help me understand who He is.

Under each layer of sadness or anger, I found another layer until I was able to relate to the sadness and anger God has felt. I found company in my misery. I felt His nearness and for the first time in days. I was more aware of the fallen nature of humanity and how it breaks the heart of Love. I wasn't relieved. Wise words didn't bring healing. We just sat in pain together, and that was just barely enough. I wasn't alone. I was no longer misun-derstood or holding back.

I cried so much. That wasn't different from any of the other days the past two months, but this time, as my tears poured from my eyes, I was sowing them into tilled ground. I was almost hopeful that someday I would reap joy. I didn't feel optimistic about the future. But I knew that if I took the seeds of my broken dreams and let them go from the storehouse into ready ground, maybe one day I would have a garden.

During my second day of falling apart in the prayer room, I ran into my good friend Peter. We met in a room off the cafe, and he sat with me in my sadness. He called me out when I was trying to put theological "bandaids" on my gaping wounds. He let me say how I felt without making it sound pretty or holy. He related with me about how much life sucks sometimes. And every few minutes he would say something that the Holy Spirit breathed on, and I would feel a little more alive.

Peter said that we have been invited to acknowledge Him in all our ways, not just the good days or tender moments (Proverbs 3:6). Acknowledge Him in the negatively-felt emotions. He suggested it might not be time for me to heal right away. It might be a time to wrestle with God. Even if I lose a hip, I'll get a new name. Then he spoke about my power in God and how remarkable I am. The enemy wants to kill me and destroy me. He wants to steal all he can so that I will turn from God. If I do, that's when he can really destroy me.

Peter said, "I would rather you endure pain than regret." And I knew God felt the same way about me. Pain proves we are alive. It strengthens us and allows opportunity for deep comfort and connection. Regret produces shame and bitterness. It opens doors for strongholds and lesser ways of living.

We have a choice. God does not force us into His love. He doesn't force Himself on us. He is not manipulating us so that we are trapped in Him. He creates a safe place for us to choose. He protects us and saves us. He comforts us and relates to us in our pain. Our faithfulness is our choice. The rest is up to God. Life will be beautiful and great, and life will be hard. God will be constant. There is no future without Him if we want Him involved. He is powerful, but He is also self-controlled. He is every light in the darkness and from Him is every good thing, even when hardly anything seems good.

Pain led me to a certain numbness—a realization of the vanity of life. What's the point of hoping if we cannot have the fullness of what Jesus died for on this side of death? Hope is the better alternative. Paul prays in Ephesians 1:18 that we would know the hope to which we have been called. We have been called to hope. It is a tree of life when fulfilled. Sow into the life that may one day be. We can stay in disappointment if we want to. But when we invite God into our disappointment, He creates a way out in time. Remember, He puts a door of hope in the valley of trouble (Hosea 2). I urge you to invite God into what you feel. Acknowledge Him in all your ways. He'll make the path straight. In Romans 8, Paul says:

> "For in this hope we were saved. But hope that is seen is no hope at all. Who hopes for what they already have? But if we hope for what we do not yet have, we wait for it patiently. In the same way, the Spirit helps us in our weakness. We do not know what we ought to pray for, but the Spirit himself intercedes for us through wordless groans."

Hope requires acknowledging what is good that is not yet. It requires patience and may involve weakness or confusion. But the Spirit, who is in us, is interceding for us (Hebrews 7:25). He prays for our faith not to fail. He groans for us. He desires that His will works in our lives for our favor.

A while back I came down with a bad sinus infection and binge-watched Once Upon a Time, a show about fairy tales meeting real life, on Netflix because I was too sick to get out of bed. At one point a character tells another, "The first step in a new beginning is imagining what's possible." As I laid miserably uncomfortable in my bed for the next two days, I couldn't shake that sentence. I was going through a significantly hopeless period and felt God nudging me to imagine what life could be. Disappointment tells us it will always be this way. Hope declares it will always get better.

In high school, a therapist told me life cycles between good and bad. I have since adopted a different perspective. Life is a kingdom advancing. Some days we may have victories, and some days we may face losses. But we aren't trapped in a circle of highs and lows. We are gaining ground until the day we are ruling and reigning with our Father for all eternity. There is a time to work through disappointment, but there is always a following time to begin dreaming again. Imagining your future with God is the first step toward hope again.

I've been disappointed by what I expected God to do for me. But there is no pain I have sustained that He has not redeemed or healed. God is generous, not withholding. We have to remember that when things are stripped away from us, He is still selflessly loving. Chasing that truth will help you find meaningful light in every heartbreak. We don't have possession or control of anything; it's all an illusion. We can only embrace what we can when we can, and then we have to let go.

This understanding felt like receiving sad news. Then I thought of hugs. These brief interactions of closeness and intimacy are followed by distance. Ending a hug is not offensive or heartbreaking. Hugs are not meant to last forever; all hugs must come to an end. I still know I am loved. The things we hold dear in this life are all only hugs. Some may last longer than others, but, sooner or later, they must end. We have to let go. We can trust we are still loved when something ends in our lives or someone leaves.

Months after this revelation, I found myself facing another big life transition. In the midst of those changes, I expressed anger to God that I have to let go of so many people in my life to step into the great things He has for me. Every time I leave a place, I feel hurt. I walk away knowing I will have to adjust friendships, experience changes in my family relational dynamics, and will inevitably have to leave some people behind. That's when I felt the Holy Spirit remind me of John 10:10, where Jesus says, "The thief comes only to steal, kill, and destroy. I have come that they may have life, and have it to the full."

He comes to bring us full lives, not to steal. He does not steal people from us or steal us from them. Believing the opposite implies cruelty in His nature, but the truth is that He is good. After gaining this understanding, I got to have an incredible conversation with one of my closest friends who assured me she intended to stick by me through the transition even though it may be hard. Later that week, I was able to have lunch with someone I had lost touch with for years. God was showing me that while things on this earth only lasts for a time, He is faithful to restore it all. He'll restore everything.

I had to have that first revelation of ending embraces to really understand the second portion of that revelation—that God doesn't steal. He deconstructed my fear of loss and change then gave my everlasting spirit peace to rest in and truth of His character to stand on. This experience reminded me that we are always learning. God is always teaching us new things, building on what He has taught us. He keeps showing us He is better than we think. There's always more of Him to love.

I don't want to live my life kicking and screaming when things come to an end. I want to love what I have had and love what I have now, looking hopefully toward what I may someday have. This is the grace I can extend to myself and everything in my life that I cherish. None of it is mine; it's all a blessing. The only things we can possess that can never be taken are faith, love, and hope.

Living for the sake of living and loving is the best we can do. Were we to live for anything other than to receive life as the gift it is, we may find burdens never intended for our shoulders, disappointment more familiar than miracles, and pressure deeply intermingled with our purpose. Live with the intent to enjoy what our generous Father has given. Burdens will be lifted, disappointment will fade away, and pressure will dissolve as life is immersed in the extravagant love of God.

Eternal Perspective

My grandfather was fully restored physically and spiritually when he passed away. God healed him completely. If we don't attempt to grasp the reality of eternity, we will miss out on the essence of what Jesus died to give us—life everlasting. In Christ, our lives last beyond death, so we cannot limit our comprehension of God's love to this momentary and fleeting life. As I walk through the grief of losing someone, I can trust God. He who redeemed my grandfather's situation to the best possible redemption will work all things together for my good as well. Until I see the goodness of God, I can believe that God is not finished with my circumstances.

We can hope for this world to be better. We can change this world, bringing pieces of heaven to earth. We can pray for the restoration of relationships and the end of injustice. These hopes are in alignment with the will of God. But we have to receive those things with open hands. Our hope, our promised land, our inheritance is Christ. He continues to give Himself to us. He has desires to heal this world but He won't force them on broken, fearful, defensive hearts. I imagine a kind father adopting a young girl who has been abused. As much as he loves her and wants to restore her, forcing his will on her will only hurt her. Love takes patience and self control. This is who God is. Love endures all things—even pain, even delayed hope.

I distance myself from heaven and the Father when I believe heaven is a place where everyone is shallowly happy and God gets everything He wants. God is not selfish. He feels brokenness, sadness, and pain, but He is not overcome. His hope is sustaining and everlasting. So He isn't deterred when you have pain to bring Him. He has pain, too. It doesn't default His perfection, it is a branch of His deep care.

You can be in pain and not be broken. You are an everlasting spirit in Christ that is perfectly loved, and you are compassionate. You're hopeful and caring. Your hope and your pain is not in vain. Trees of life are growing with every dream and every tear. I imagine God has promised a tree of life that will last for all of eternity and maybe I'll see it when I get to heaven. Every day for eternity I'll walk past it and remember the hurt and hope I felt. It'll be alright—not because this life is easy, but because our lives are eternal.

There's something on the other side of death, and that's hope. Even if you don't want it or you don't know what it is, you know it's there. You can always choose to believe, even if you don't feel like it. Some day your feelings will catch up. There is no end to the End, and in the End there is good. Even the finality of death is not permanent.

God says in Revelation 21 (ESV), "I am making all things new." He comes to redeem it all in the end. He makes it all new because He is good. We serve a God of redemption, of vengeance, of wisdom, of love. Put your hope in God when you have no vision for what is to come. He won't let you down. He can make everything new.

Signals of hope are like sparks of magic. In a discipleship meeting with one of my girls, we passed a three-legged dog, and I started laughing. For years, three-legged dogs have been a sign from God to me that He is engaged in my life. I don't even remember where it first started. I really love three-legged dogs. I've found just a handful of times in life I'll be talking to God about something and pass a three-legged dog. It's a funny reminder to me that God is real and present. It's a reminder to believe that God knows what I love and knows where I am.

Clouds have also been a signal of hope for me in the past couple of years. In really special moments, I've noticed the skies and seen beautiful canvases of clouds above me. Throughout the Word, clouds are used in reference to the glory or light of God.

They symbolize His provision, protection, and power. When I look up at the clouds, I'm reminded of God's intentionality and creativity. Find the things between you and God that remind you of His character and that give you a reason to keep believing. Watch Him come through for you. Watch Him reveal Himself to you through silly things and signs that hold special meaning.

Many circumstances we face in life will appear hopeless. Jesus died for us to have another option, a better truth. This is our hope every time. What does God have to say about your situation? What does He see when He looks at it? Whether it's a miraculous thought, perspective shift, or change of behavior, God redeems. We can lift our eyes to the hills and find help (Psalm 121). Hope is not easy. It is a war against bitterness and complacency. Sometimes hope will feel like the most ridiculous, unnatural exercise of spirituality. But it can remain through anything forever (1 Corinthians 13:13). Hope will outlast our suffering and our disappointment. It will outlive our brokenness and pain. It will overcome our hopelessness through the grace of God.

The Problem of Pain

I've wrestled with the problem of pain and have yet to find any solutions, but I have found some peace in pieces of truth. The first was when one of my leaders told me, "to love God is to love God." He was encouraging me to believe our love for God should never be dependent on if things go our way or we get what we want; it should be independent and strong enough to sustain us on its own. God's love for us is not conditional, so why should our love for Him be?

Another leader of mine once said connection should never be up for negotiation when a healthy relationship goes through healthy conflict. I have used my affection for God as a bargaining chip when I experience hard times, as if He deserves for me to withhold my love when I am upset with Him or my circumstances. The love that we have received and are capable of giving goes beyond this pettiness. Our choice to love God remains constant, regardless of the situations we experience. We can decide to engage or disengage with Him in our struggles. But to truly love Him is to choose to love Him despite the lack of feelings or trust. In the end, we will find that He is faithful and loving. This doesn't protect us from the sting of pain, but Love has arms for us to fall into when we are hurting.

Another truth I learned about pain came from one of my good friends, Tori. She taught me that being sad doesn't mean your season is bad. If your heart is soft, that is good. God cares more about the condition of your heart than the circumstances of your surroundings. Emotions are part of your soul; they are not of your spirit. You are capable of experiencing joy in sadness and peace in anger. You can trust God even in doubt because your feelings are not the essence of who you are.

I had a moment with God in a prayer chapel singing about being desperate for Him. I've tasted and seen, and I didn't want Him. I told Him I wished I felt differently but I was so tired of singing the same songs without feeling anything. For weeks I would show up to services, pray, and worship without feeling filled up by the time I left. I was disappointed that I wasn't encountering Him the way I wanted to. But I kept showing up because I knew He would help me understand what made me feel like there was a divide between us. I was desperate for a touch from Him. I chose to love by His grace and He encountered me with love. I felt Him reminding me of His kindness. He is faithful. He didn't reject me because my capacity to love didn't match His. He brought me into more. As I sang, I was filled with thankfulness for my relationship with God.

In the moments I glimpse the coming pleasure beyond the pain, I only see God. I can recognize Him in all I've been through, and I'm ready to be in love again. With people, with life, with Him. I see it was all for good. One day my body and soul will come into more alignment with the Spirit in me that is eternal. Then I will be restored. I know that day is coming. The moments I can acknowledge that hope are just as real as moments of pain.

Peace has come from realizing that sometimes thankfulness softens the pain. We can't heal our own bodies, souls, or spirits. We are fully dependent on God, and pain is one of the most powerful reminders of that. But He will heal all, and that's what I hold onto. The morning will tempt us to believe there are no new mercies. God speaks a better word. Pain reveals the brokenness our satisfaction keeps us ignorant of in the world. Even pain He can use for good.

Pain is Pain

A somewhat dismal perspective on the world holds a truth that has managed to bring little bits of peace for me: everything is meaningless. This ecclesiastical schema is interlaced with a thread of hope: our lives will never be fulfilled here, but we were made for a life, for a world, for a love that will fulfill us. Held in tension with the hope of eternity, it's a great reminder that if I miss out in this life, I'm not at a loss. There's more for me in the life to come. The pain that we endure is temporary. For all the misery and heartbreak it brings– it's just pain. Pain is as reliable as the morning. No one makes it out of this life alive (except maybe Elijah and Enoch). The world is put into a clearer perspective when I recognize that truth and I'm motivated to live as fully as I can within the limitations our mortality has defined for us. However, I definitely need to keep these thoughts in check to avoid falling into a deep, dark depression while considering the meaninglessness of it all.

One of the most compelling truths I have discovered in my pain is that just because God is powerful doesn't mean He is cruel. A twisted and self-serving understanding of authority has conditioned us to believe that power and cruelty are inevitably interwoven. God is above that. He is kind and works all things together for our good. Jesus, the physical incarnation of the invisible Father, revealed what a kind ruler is like. I have seen the evidence in my own life. I have seen God's kindness everywhere as I heal. He doesn't leave us. He is faithful. I've yet to find a way to explain why bad things happen. I have my theories, but I am unconvinced they are anywhere close to complete. I have heard others share compelling arguments, but have yet to be convinced they reveal the full picture.

My counselor corrected me for categorizing my emotions as "positive" and "negative," "good" and "bad." He prefers the terms "pleasant" and "unpleasant" because all emotions serve good purposes. When we feel unpleasant emotions as a result of unpleasant situations, we can keep in mind that good is not forced away. God works all things together for our good, which is so kind, and we can see Him do it. We feel anger, unpleasant as it seems, and know that something is wrong. We feel hurt and know that things are not as they ought to be. Pain indicates a problem, and we can choose to acknowledge the need for a solution.

During one particularly brutal meltdown, I felt God say to me, "You are the beauty in your pain." I was so lost in my hurt that I couldn't see any beauty in it, and finding the bright side has been a lifeline in my survival. I thought of the people in my life who I have watched suffer and how much love in my heart I held for them. I thought of how beautiful their tears were and their relentless, desperate pursuit of life was. In the midst of our brokenness and despair, God sees beauty in us. When we aren't the ones hurting, it's easy to see that our suffering loved ones are worth fighting for, worth hoping for, and worth continuing on for. I've seen all kinds of people and all kinds of hurt feelings— broken and ugly and guilty, but God calls them beautiful and makes them so.

When things change, it can be painful. Letting go of what we are used to is painful. Transitions can be painful. Adjusting to a new way of life can be painful. Painful events can cause ripple effects throughout our lives that hurt. So many small moments throughout any given day may remind us of a recent tragic event. A song on the radio, a word we read, a sign we see can take us back to the pain we felt and the loss we endure.

Sometimes good change can cause pain. Moving to a different city or starting a new job is initially uncomfortable. We can feel like we don't have a place and that we have nearly endless work ahead of us to create a life we enjoy. Pain isn't always the result of something bad. Neutral and even good things can also hurt us. Vaccines, honest conversations, and pain receptors lead us toward healthier lives. We have to learn not to despise our pain but to respect it for what it is.

I lived in fear of pain for most of my life. I wanted to avoid it so badly because it hurts so deeply. When pain would waltz into my world, I would spiral into a dark cloud of "whys" and feel deeply unsettled. I was so afraid of pain until I realized that pain is not the end of me, nor could it ever be. I only get stronger with every hit I sustain. I have a foundation to secure me now. My hope in God keeps me from being shaken in the worst storms. Only death will ever kill me, and even then, death can only have my body. Pain is not as big and scary as I had made it out to be. We heal from hurt, we grow from death, we are restored from loss, and we are redeemed from mortality.

Pain is all over and throughout the world. If I choose to ignore it, it's my loss because I'm a healer. So are you. When we come in close contact with pain, we get to step into more of our identities as children of God. The Holy Spirit in us is able to work through us to bring peace to chaos and mending to brokenness. As I acknowledge my own pain, I open the door to a path of healing. As I step into the pain of the world, I lead others toward restoration. Our blissful ignorance to pain keeps us from meeting a hurting world with redemptive love. I think it's worth it to experience pain so that we can help people in theirs.

The pastor of a nearby church once told me, "I would choose to hurt deeply if the only alternative was to never love, and it is." Loving is accompanied by pain. Love is not rivaled by pain; love always prevails. But it is shadowed by pain in the light cast on our humanity. Love is never weighed and found wanting; it is worth the pain that ensues from giving our hearts away, altogether or in pieces. The only way to securely protect ourselves from pain is to reject love, both giving and receiving, the very thing we were made for.

When I've been in pain, I've been drawn toward ugly feelings of bitterness, resentment, anger, aggression, fear, and so on. I'm sure you can relate. Pain can bring out the darker sides of us. It dawned on me as I was meeting with a minister in Charlotte once that God should be a better friend to us than the insidious reactions rooted in pain. If I'm more familiar with a voice of bitterness in my head than the voice of Truth, I'm missing out on a blessing God has purchased for me. If I'm spending more time wallowing in resentment than resting in peace, I'm missing out again. Jesus called us friends in John 15. We should spend our time with Him, becoming like Him as we do. The selfishness of our self-preservation will begin to dissolve as we let Jesus encourage us, strengthen us, and lead us through our pain. With the hope of Jesus, we will receive healing and restoration. In the meantime, we reconcile our pain and limitations with the promise of eternal life.

Created

This world is far beyond my understanding. The universe is incomprehensible. I most often become angry with God when I don't understand, and that most often occurs due to my limited knowledge of time. I try not to believe in superstitions, but if there were one I could fall for it would be this: bad things come in threes. Somehow one thing in my life can go wrong, and two others quickly follow. Then I'm okay again. Of course, it's not entirely dependable (because it's not real), but it seems to be that way.

For example, my friend's sister was tragically killed one weekend. The next day, a celebrity death took over the headlines of every social media platform. The following day, another friend lost a loved one. Then I heard of no other deaths for weeks. Another time someone texted me a hurtful message out of the blue, an hour later I found out I didn't get a job I wanted, and a few hours after that I got denied from a graduate school I applied to. The next day, life was easy.

Maybe I see things in three's because I want to or maybe there's something to my bad trio theory. Either way, I have found myself curious about the timing of life. Why can't life unfold according to my ten-year plan? I quit making ten-year plans. Why does it take so long to recover from some pain? When do I get to start living the life I dreamed of? How long will certain memories haunt me?

The answers to all of these are fully known to One and only One. He is the Spirit of Truth, so I can trust that all truth is found in and known by Him (John 14). God knows what I should do with my sad memories and distorted perceptions, just like He knows how each moment of my life will open up before me and the days I will see my dreams come true. The same hands that formed my mind separated from the day from night. He called it all "good." So as I wrestle with questions about my perception of time, I remain confident in the kindness of His intentionality.

Imagination

God is able to do more than we imagine (Ephesians 3:20), so I like to ask, what have I imagined? I love to have my head in the clouds. Part of hope looks like revving up our mind's imagination stations and seeing what possibilities we can create. Childish as it may appear to be, imagination is the mark of innovators and trailblazers. They come up with ideas that are new or upcycle old ideas and take a chance. We can be innovators in the faith. Imagine what God has for your life, your family, your ministry, then go for it because God can do abundantly more than even that.

Imagination can sustain our passion and our hope. In the movie, Hook, starring Robin Williams, the characters imagine a feast for themselves. They change their experience by indulging in hopeful, creative thought. I think one of the biggest roadblocks to our faith is that we keep fun out. God created your mind. He created your ability to imagine. Why waste it? Why grow out of it? It will keep you young.

Fantasy can quickly turn on you, which is why you should always mind your mind. Lust, anger, and anxiety will take over in a heartbeat if you aren't paying attention. Think of all the arguments you've played out in your head throughout your lifetime. What if you could get that time back? Would you spend it the same way? Why spend your thoughts on hate when you could exchange them for new dreams? Jesus suggested even our private thoughts are accountable to Him when He gave the sermon on the Mount (Matthew 5:28).

I have had many friends tell me they have experienced extended periods of anxiety, typically accompanied with dark imaginations. Some envision themselves getting into a car accident as they're driving down the road; others may fear a terminal diagnosis on their way to routine check ups. Anxiety can warp your imagination to produce some very scary worst-case scenarios, but anxiety has no right to rule your mind. It must submit to Christ just like any other thought. You are empowered to make it do so. Anxiety says, "You're not safe" and specifically, "Your future is not safe."

In moments when anxiety hits and you can ease the physiological responses, do so. But whether or not you can quiet your body, you can always ask yourself, "What is threatening me and what does God say?" Remember that God is your Defender with a purpose for your life and a prosperous future for you without intended harm (Jeremiah 29:11). When it comes to anxiety, the plan isn't to get rid of it but to experience a biologically necessary and appropriate amount. Anxiety is a survival mechanism. You're not defective if you experience anxiety. You just need to remember anxiety is under the Lordship of Christ. Instead of living anxiously, you are invited to let the peace of God guard your heart (Philippeans 4:7) and imagine what is lovely and pure, noble and right (Philippeans 4:8).

Anger will destroy our God-given relationships if it is not kept in check. Like anxiety, we shouldn't do away with it completely but submit it to Christ. Anger in the voice of our internal justice system alerting us when something is not right. Dwelling on hateful thoughts is not an innocent crime (Matthew 5:22). Rather than out-bursting or suppressing anger, we should train ourselves not to sin in our anger. Sinning in anger looks like gossip, ill-intentions, revenge-plotting, fits of rage, snide remarks, and so on.

I was brilliant at suppressing anger under the guise of graciousness. It wasn't until I was experiencing severe grief that I noticed how short my temper had become. People frustrated me constantly. I felt like an exposed nerve. I took some time to reflect on what was off. Identifying what was not right allowed me to ask God what would be right moving forward. I can't change the people around me, who were mostly doing nothing extraordinarily wrong, but I could change my reactions. Once I was honest with myself about the judgments I was passing on people, I was able to choose humility and embrace the justice system of God. Selfless confrontation paired with generous grace came from trusting that God is just. I didn't have to hold back a river of anger inside anymore. God made it all right when He promised to make all things right. I found rest in the patient assurance that God would come through for me. I felt more capacity to love people after processing my anger.

Lust is a tricky beast. I have talked to and been one of the many girls who dream up an entire future around a boy we've rarely or never talked to. Being a daydreamer, it was not unusual for me to mentally check out in classes or big meetings. I would waste those times playing back memories of romance I'd experienced, witnessed, or desired. Then, by the grace of God, it dawned on me that lust is a big lie. We spend all this time and mental energy on relationships that aren't real. We get dissatisfied with real life because we are investing in a delusion. We set ourselves up for disappointment and dishonor human beings made in the image of God. The conviction brought me so much freedom because the temptation was incredibly less appealing.

I've spent too much time using my imagination to fill my head with garbage. There is a God whose love is more fearfully wonderful than anything I've ever known and who created the heavens more expansively massive than I could ever fully discover. I'd rather fill my head with what is true. I would rather dream of what is pure. The fruit of what I sow will be wild and miraculous because I will have possibilities I would have never unearthed if I chose to dwell on sinful thoughts.

Memory

Our memories are magic. They can carry us through time and space to our best days, worst experiences, and anywhere in between. God, being omnipresent, is there for all of it. Our histories are riddled with hidden treasures. Finding God in our memories can help bring closure and facilitate intimacy. He has an opinion about everything you can remember in your life.

God was there in the tainted memories—the ones that make your stomach turn, the ones that come out of nowhere, and the ones that get triggered by the smallest things. God was there in the sweetest moments that are now covered in bitterness. He saw your joy, and He knew your future. He rejoiced with you, and now He mourns with you. He mourned with you, and now He rejoices with you. He doesn't black out the parts of your life you want to forget. He wants to show His faithfulness and His engagement in every one. Ask Him where He was, what He felt, what He has to say now.

When I'm angry about something that occurred in the past, I don't care if my feelings are logical and make sense. I'm angry and I need someone to validate my feelings. Then it hit me: why do I expect my memories to make sense if I don't expect myself to make sense? We can let go of the need for rationale. It shouldn't always matter if we can fully understand why things happened the way they did. Our most prevalent memories may not yet have explanations, but don't let offense take over. Sometimes I get so eager to understand that I forget understanding is not always necessary. It is good to wait on the Lord. He will tell you what you need to know when you need to know it. As you search your memories with God, release Him from the expectation of validation and let Him affirm you how He wants to. Remember, He is kind.

We can reshape our minds by changing our perspectives. I coach clients in developing optimism and get to watch the progress as they transform from pessimistic people to hopeful people. Through simple development strategies like monitoring self talk and adapting expectations, they re-navigate and create new pathways in their minds. Sifting through significant memories and asking God for His perspective on them or where He was during them can help us view the present and future in a softer, brighter light.

Integration

The beauty of existing as spiritual beings is that we can integrate God into everything. Including God in my life doesn't feel like extra work; it feels like embracing an entire portion of myself that is otherwise often neglected. Immersing our minds in God provides a sense of security and unending love. We are invited to abide in Him, to remain in Him (John 15:4). Connecting with Him as we read the Bible, watch movies, experience nature, until He is in everything brings us to hope more, dream more, see more come to pass, and produce more thankfulness.

Someone once told me, "If we are aware, at least we have a chance." Becoming aware of the areas of our lives that appear distant from God grants us the opportunity to fill the gap with willingness. My mind is more at peace when I abide by the instruction of Scripture. My faith is more evident when I am at peace in my mind. My life is more attractive when my faith is evident. This is not in an effort to attract people to me but to attract people to the Light of God that I reflect when I let His peace guard my mind.

Schema

Schemas are worldviews; they are the lenses through which we perceive reality. My schema can be corrupted by evil as easily as it can be enveloped in goodness. I don't believe that we were originally meant to know good and evil. Before the fall of man, we were supposed to live in the fullness of God's goodness. I believe God foresaw the fall and expected us to cope with the consequences of our sin, but He never desired for us to know good and evil. Similar to how parents don't want their children to be exposed to crime, God asked Adam and Eve not to eat from the Tree of Knowledge of Good and Evil. But we do know evil just like we know good, and we also have a choice in what we perceive as evil and good.

A clear divide exists between the two, but I think in our naiveté we categorize people and places as good or evil when there can be both good and evil in almost everything. There's as much sin in church conferences as downtown bars because our righteousness is as filthy rags, yet still we act like we are better than nonbelievers. The difference is in the direction of the heart. In churches, we should be encouraged to repent from sin, whereas in bars, we are tempted to ignore conviction. Instead, let there be a flood of justice in both places (Amos 5:24). Under the new covenant, we can depend on God again rather than our own principles of righteousness.

We don't want to just view the world through a schema of religious Christianity but of who Christ has revealed Himself to be through Scripture and our intimate relationships with Him. Writing off places or people because they appear to be evil only removes your option to bring goodness into the situation. My mom often references Titus 1:15 saying, "to the pure all things are pure." She encourages me to find God in everything and be an active agent in the redemption of the world. So when I go into bars with friends, I look for opportunities to connect with loved ones rather than look for love from strangers. When I go into churches, I look for ways to minister to people rather than judge the ministry of others from a self-created pedestal.

We can identify our schemas by studying the made-up scenarios we play in our minds. If I catch myself imagining I'm telling a friend she's selfish and careless, I can pause and decipher what's really going on. I'd probably notice there's some unresolved conflict. Maybe I'm feeling threatened or unseen by our interactions and feel insecure about it. Now I have the option to ask God for peace and open up a gentle conversation with my friend. We respond based on what we think we know, so it's important we know the truth of what's going on both in our minds and in reality. This is self awareness.

The purpose of self awareness is to be able to connect better with the world around us, not to spend our lives looking inside ourselves. We need to organize our minds so that we can be present for others. Breaking habits of old thought patterns may take a while, and establishing new habits can be just as time-consuming. But as the years go by, you'll find yourself more engaged in the moment and more in tune with yourself. I know because that's my testimony. When I read my journal from the years before I started intentionally taking thoughts captive and replacing truth with lies, it's almost as if a different person was writing in my penmanship. In renewing my mind, I have learned now to exercise my rights in my new life as a child of God.

Dreams

I've had dreams in the night since I was a child. During some months of my life, I have had dreams more than others, but it's rare that I'll go a night without remembering any dreams. Growing up, my family would sit around the breakfast table and take turns sharing our dreams with one another. A few family members of mine even began to learn about dream interpretation, which is where my foundation for the gift was formed.

Dreams are mysterious. The emotional part of the brain produces dreams, not the rational part of the brain, according to my binge night of The Mind, Explained. Our dreams are combinations of our fears and our experiences. When I was younger, a guy I knew was convinced he was going to marry one of my friends because he had been dreaming about her. My assumption was that he had been thinking about her a lot throughout the day, so she became an icon in his sleep. They never got married.

Some dreams are messages from God that He can speak to us through, like the dreams of Joseph in Genesis. Some dreams are from the enemy intended to bring terror, but God can speak through those, too. Most of my dreams are from my subconscious. God can speak through those, but they may just amount to a bunch of nonsense at times. Typically when I wake up, I can sense the significance of the dream and that determines whether or not I spend much time deciphering it. A significant dream will replay in my thoughts throughout the day or maybe be suddenly recounted as the result of something similar taking place, like seeing a person who was in the dream shortly after.

Dreams from my subconscious help me understand what I'm feeling before I've been able to fully recognize it in my conscious thoughts throughout the day. In a transition period of my life, I dreamed I was aging out of foster care while other younger children I was attached to were getting reunited with their families. As I wrote out the dream in my journal the next morning, I was able to acknowledge my feelings of being passed over for opportunities and forced to let go of loved ones.

Dreams from God both align with Scripture and contain revelatory information that would be impossible for us to know through natural means. They usually compel us to pray or take action in an expression of God's love and care. Years ago I dreamed someone I knew was moving to China. I found out a few days later the person I dreamed about had just talked to his church about moving to China, and he actually moved there soon after. When I woke up from the dream, I not only had information I couldn't have known apart from God's revelation, I also felt urged to pray for the man. That was the evidence that the dream was from God in that instance.

As you pay attention to your dreams, you'll be able to learn where your dreams are coming from. Dreams from your subconscious will be results of your current feelings, thoughts, hopes, and fears. Dreams from the enemy will be perverse and evil. Dreams from God will be full of meaning and insight. This is not to say that dreams from God will be pretty, dreams from the enemy will be ugly, and dreams from ourselves will be somewhere in between. As you're learning to decipher all your significant dreams, take them to God in prayer. He can guide you in understanding all you need to know and applying that knowledge to your waking life.

Lucid dreaming is one of my favorite abilities of the human mind. I've been inconsistently capable of it since I was a child. It's a rare but exciting occurrence for me. Lucid dreaming is when, in the midst of a dream, you gain awareness that you are dreaming by waking your frontal cortex and you can begin influencing the events of your dream. Some of the most stressful periods of my life were accompanied by a series of puzzling identical dreams that I would solve in sleep as soon as my waking conflict was resolved. I can't control when these happen, but they're frustrating, challenging, fascinating gifts from God. If you don't dream, that's not a bad thing. I think you could ask God for dreams and experience them more. If you do dream, see how much fun you can have with it.

I mentioned that some dreams we have come from the enemy, but God can speak through them. I am no stranger to nightmares. A dream from the enemy leaves a residue of darkness and fear of evil when I wake. The earliest dream I can recall was a nightmare, and I will still have dreams scary enough to jolt me awake in bed.

Although the enemy uses dreams to insight fear, I don't have to stay afraid. What the enemy intends for evil, God uses for good. When I have a nightmare, I just dismiss it when I wake up. If a particular scene stays in my mind, I pray about why it won't leave and ask God what He has to say about it. The fear cannot last when I am quieted with the love of God. God is a great Father, which means He knows how to help me sleep in peace.

A while back, I dreamed a large fox with massive claws and teeth was trying to kill me. I was shaken when I woke up until I realized I was actually not in danger of a gigantic fox eating me. Still, the dream stuck in my mind. As I prayed about it, I felt the Holy Spirit impress Song of Solomon 2, specifically the verse that says, "catch for us the foxes that ruin the vineyard." I felt God reminding me to ask Him for help with my fears of taking "life from my garden" or purpose from my existence. Even though the dream was scary, God used it for my good.

In interpreting dreams, I don't take myself too seriously. I depend heavily on my personal associations for meaning. The color white represents purity to me, cars tend to be about my ministry, and my dad is often the embodiment of the Father. Repeated dreams usually indicate importance, and dreams with bombs infer urgency or timeliness. As you notice trends in your own dreams, write down what you think it means. Take your best guess, asking God for wisdom, and see if it applies to your life. If it doesn't right away, it may in the future.

I consult friends and Scripture when the conclusions aren't apparent, but where sense cannot be found, I trust God will speak to me in other ways. I don't want to get so carried away with my dreams that I miss out on my life or the many ways God communicates with me. They are gifts I choose to be thankful for without over-glorifying. Dreams are one of many ways God can speak to us. As we grow in hearing Him through our dreams, we must remember to seek His voice through the entire process because that's the whole point.

Time is a Tool

My discipler from Wesley and I were discussing time on the way to a movie about time travel. She recalled a scene from Wonder Woman when Diana asks Steve about his watch and is amused that he would let a small, man-made object dictate his daily life. Time is a tool God gave us to help us understand and interact in the world. I don't have to give it more authority than that.

Throughout college, I struggled with the concept of time. I wondered why God did and didn't do things when I thought He would. The permanence of some things like death, severe injuries, and relationships falling out scared me. The urgency in Scripture that Jesus and other New Testament writers spoke with confused me. Time felt like a mysterious concept controlling and encompassing everything. That's when I realized I was idolizing time. I was attributing power to it that belonged to God. God is omnipresent; He is both outside of and with us in time. Time is a construct developed to help us understand the change around us —the rhythms of life. For us, we experienced a beginning and, in some ways, there will be an end when we leave this earth. But beyond us, there was no beginning and there is no end with God. Exalting time above the One "who was, who is, and who is to come" can only lead us into fear, but submitting our time to God breaks the dam for everlasting love to rush in.

The most basic truth concerning time I needed to remember was that we love God because He first loved us. He is always first. I often run into the problem of time. It's okay. I am allowed to press in for more knowledge and move on when I lose curiosity. Our pursuit of knowledge should lead us into more peace and excitement rather than anxiety or frustration.

Our minds are time machines. They are constantly retracing the past to predict the future. Every moment is an opportunity. Use the time machine—don't let it use you. You're not trapped in it. You are given it as a gift to use. You can predict your future because, with God, you can create your future. You get little gifts called dreams and passions that will light your way. You have moments in your personal history that are leading up to something. Note the clues, and let your hope grow.

His Timing

Time is often man's attempt to comprehend aspects of creation we don't understand and to reach for answers in circumstances that bring us pain and impatience. We wonder why children die or how long ago the earth was formed. We wonder how long the sun will last and when we will enter the next stages of our lives. God has promised to make everything beautiful in it's time (Ecclesiastes 3:11). I think that's the best we can know for certain.

Predestination is a topic that comes up often in my discipleship meetings with my girls. Though I cannot offer them absolute answers, I can offer perspective and a listening ear. Before any conversation of the sort, I like to remind my girls that focusing too intently on theological arguments about predestination and free will trip people up. I think there is enough evidence on both sides to believe whichever helps you know God better. I personally believe they are both true. I have not fully figured out yet how that can be possible, but I can tell you what I've learned so far.

My friend Emily and I were driving through the Blue Ridge Mountains fleshing out our thoughts on predestination and free will. Graduate school was my plan for my next step in life, but I wasn't sure which graduate school I would attend. She asked, "Do you think God has a specific graduate school that you are destined to attend?"

The thought I expressed was that, according to His foreknowledge, I am predestined for things when I am in Christ (1 Peter 1:2). As I pursue God, I receive all God has for me that He knew long before I knew Him I would want. In that sense, I am predestined. I also believe that I have the freedom of choice in my life. I think I could feel a call to a particular graduate school and go to another instead and be outside the desired will of God. But should I return to God, He could restore all I lost in going to a school He wasn't calling me to. Jonah was called to Nineveh and chose to run toward Tarshish, then he ended up in Nineveh. He chose his own will over the will of God but ended up in the place God had intended for him all the same.

I told Emily I couldn't decide if time was a fabric being sewn together with every moment we live or if it were a quilt already sewn together that God is tracing His finger along. But I do know that God is not bound by time. I think our lives are both made and being made by the Author and Perfecter of our faith. I am persuaded by John 3:16 to believe that I was one of the "whoevers" invited to love God and chose to, so now I have eternal life. Regardless of if I am right or wrong, I will love God. If I stand before Him someday and realize He had predestined every step, every breath, every choice my whole life, He will be no less worthy and no less loved. And if He applauds every choice I made to follow Him in my own doing, He will be no less sovereign and no less powerful.

Power Over Time

Your prayers make a difference. We experience life and God in seasons, but God is outside of and with us time. He is bigger than time. When we begin to grasp that, we access power to more hope and more knowledge.

Our relationship with the Trinity is difficult to understand within the constraints of time. But we were made for eternity, so we can find clues written on our hearts and hidden in our relationships. Sometimes we pray to the Father because that's how Jesus taught us to in Matthew 6. Sometimes we pray to the Son. Personally, that's the kind of prayer I learned to pray before meals. My siblings and I would take turns saying the blessing, "Thank you, Jesus, for this food. I pray that it will bless our bodies and hearts. In Jesus' name, Amen." At times we pray to the Holy Spirit. A song that was popular for years in contemporary churches was directed to Him saying, "Holy Spirit, You are welcome here." He is Three in One, which is just about as confusing as it can get.

God has many names, and I don't believe there is one name more right to pray to than others. He has revealed Himself to us in different ways at different times. We won't truly grasp the vastness of His identity this side of eternity. But praying to Him alone can change the outcomes of events. We see testimonies of this power all throughout Scripture and have no reason to believe things must be different today. We do not only pray to receive a desired result. In the extravagance of God's kindness to us, we may see our world change as a result of our growing relationships with God.

God responds to our prayers, which allows Jesus to help us in the unfolding of events we call "time." 1 John 5:14-15 says:

> "This is the confidence we have in approaching God: that if we ask anything according to His will, He hears us. And if we know that He hears us—whatever we ask —we know that we have what we asked of Him."

Have confidence approaching God and pray big. Prayer is the closest thing to childhood fairytale power we can attain, and it's even better than that kind of magic because it's a gift from God. James 4:2-3 tells us we have not because we ask not. I cannot account for why some prayers lack the results we asked for, but I can encourage you to ask with courage. Ask on the chance that you could change what the forces of nature have established. The Creator of it all has lent His ear to us.

Be Present

We fight to stay present, and it is a fight. Between past, present, and future, present has the shortest duration, and is also the stage in which we spend the most time. We are constantly accumulating pasts and stepping into our futures, but constantly present. In the time it took to read the beginning of this sentence, we have already lost a present moment. Being engaged with right now requires mindfulness and releases us from anxiety. Just thinking about how quickly our pasts are growing can induce fear, and looking at the unknown future may have the same effect.

Instead, we can break out of the bondage of time with thankfulness for the current moment, current feelings, current history, and current hope for us. Thankfulness is an acknowledgement of what is pleasant and good with what we have in front of us. Control is an illusion, as is possession. We think we have possession of loved ones and control over our circumstances at times. In reality, we cannot hold onto anything. Being present is most effectively accomplished by recognizing what good is in the moment and thanking God for it all.

For a few days the phrase, "let a good thing be a good thing" kept circulating in my mind. I felt like God was encouraging me to be thankful for what good things I have and let go of what they could be, what they should be, what they aren't. For example, there was a mission trip I went on that was difficult, but I enjoyed the ministry I got to do there. I felt like I wasn't being led to go back, but it hurt to not sign back up because I missed the people I met there. I could have responded with bitterness toward God and dwelt on the past. I could have responded with anger toward God and dealt with discontentment when the trip rolled around. But instead I felt God leading me to see the past trip as a good thing and trust that He has other good things coming my way. This allows me the opportunity to be present in my thankfulness and trust in God's goodness toward me.

Being present does not always buffer against the impending future. Especially in seasons of transition, ignoring the days ahead isn't beneficial. I would argue that we weren't created to be fully present at all times because our brains are constantly trying to predict the cucumber. Read that sentence again. Did it surprise you that cucumber was at the end? That's probably because your brain had predicted it would say "future."

A key I've found to work in my favor is being wise about the future, but not anxious. There's a subtle but vital difference between wisdom and fear. Wisdom is going to shore when someone yells "SHARK!" at the beach; fear is not swimming in a pool at night because I think a shark could be in there. When considering the future, it is good to dream and plan. Wisdom is having a savings account, having a vision for your life, having goals you set. Fear is hoarding money, becoming inflexible in your plans, or filling up your time with busyness to avoid the risk it takes to actually live life. There's nothing to fear in your future. God is in every bit of it. Be wise, but not anxious. Then your present won't be filled with tense shoulders, rampant thoughts, and an unusually high heart rate. You can be prepared without being wholly invested in a day you cannot yet touch no matter how hard you try.

Boredom

Speaking of busyness, have you ever been bored? So many students I meet with hate being bored. They do anything they can to avoid it. I started embracing boredom a few years ago when I learned that boredom is an avenue for developing creativity and empathy. Some of my wildest ideas and most thoughtful conversations come from being bored. If you can choose to embrace boring moments, you'll feel naturally inclined to create a better moment.

I sit through a lot of teachings and meetings. They're not all fun or exciting. When I notice myself getting bored, that's my reminder that I am empowered to make the experience what I want it to be. Jessica Longino, the leader who shared the beautiful re-telling of the Gospel, taught me that creativity thrives within limits. I loved that. Pride hinders me from receiving everything a moment has to offer. In boring meetings, my pride suggests there are better things I can do with my time. When I choose humility, creativity reminds me that I can learn from anyone and anything. If I'm not interested in the topic, I pay attention to how the speaker communicates. In boring moments of solitude, my insecurity can start to kick in saying I'm not worth connecting with. I can disengage with life and go to social media to find pseudo-intimacy, or I can engage with the boredom and develop my self worth. Or stare out the window and notice things I overlook on a typical day, read, draw, write, or find another activity I enjoy.

Embracing boredom is one of the most beneficial things we can do to stay present because if you can choose to be present when there's not much to be present for, you can be present in anything. You can endure boredom if you set your mind to it, and it will stretch your capacity for boredom. Exercising the muscles of your capacity will cause you to be more present.

Rested

Pixar's Up, the story of an ambitious boy and a grumpy widower's journey to South America in a floating house, was one of my favorite movies when it came out. Besides all the beautiful scenes and touching storyline, I thought it was hilarious. In one scene, Russell (the young wilderness explorer) is escorting Carl (the bitter old widower) through the jungle. Russell complains about how tired he is as he falls face-flat on the ground saying, "I don't want to walk anymore." His weak body is dragged along the ground as the rope attached to his backpack is pulled along by Carl. I laughed and laughed the first time I saw it. Some days I feel that tired. Some weeks, like midterm weeks, are filled with hours worth of meetings back-to-back with students telling me they're tired enough to quit. And let me tell you, that is tiring.

But I don't want to live a zombie-life. I want to live to the rhythm of rest. In simpler times, I'm the girl who goes to bed at ten or eleven, sleeps eight hours, then dances out of bed to the song of the birds outside my window. I drink green tea instead of black coffee to avoid caffeine crashes. I work really hard, then I leave work at work. In more difficult times, rest becomes a top priority because I believe we need rest to recover well. Finding a productive rhythm of rest to live by may take some time and readjusting but, let me tell you, it's amazing.

Dos and Don'ts

Life-giving rest is vital to incorporate into our routines. Through trial and error I've determined what personally qualifies as life giving rest and what does not. This doesn't mean the "dos" are fool-proof and the "don'ts" are detrimental. It's just a guide I've created for myself from my experiences that hopefully will aid you in discovering your own.

When I first pursued self-care in high school, I decided to make a list of activities I could do that range in effort level, interests, and time consumption. Instead of choosing between napping or binging Netflix when I needed rest, I had more options. I would go for walks, make fun snacks, read books, learn new languages, and so on. I came up with a hundred different activities that would revive me for my down time. I've also helped my girls create their own lists of things to do in free time that will relax them or allow them to leisurely produce things.

TV and social media are addictions that I mistake for rest. I once had an Oceans movie marathon with a couple friends. It seemed like a great idea and a fun way to chill on a Saturday. We watched all the movies, but by the end of the day, I was drained. My brain felt dull, my body felt tired. I didn't want to sit or lay down anymore, but I was exhausted. I had been so out of the habit of binging on media that I realized how harmful it actually is. I'm all for movies and TV shows (if you didn't notice already). But I don't think excessive media is a refreshing or life-giving resource.

Being inside all the time will also drain the life out of me. I try to be intentional to get fresh air every day. Sometimes that's just enjoying the walk from my car to work and back. Most days that looks like taking my dog on a run around the neighborhood. At times I've played baseball in the parking lot at work or hit a tennis ball around with some friends. You can enjoy the outdoors in any non-life-threatening weather if you have the right attitude. Even sitting on my back porch in the evenings with a cup of tea is a life-giving activity for me.

In more difficult times of life, being outside isn't always enjoyable. All the colors seem dimmer and the sounds are more agitating. But as I heal, I notice the greens in trees and the wind blowing through the leaves. The little things about the world around me remind me of God's creativity. I think about how He said it was all good, and I can agree.

Sleep: Prioritizing sleep is a huge "do." One of my girls said it changed her life when she started getting eight hours of sleep each night. Figure out what you need to do to get the sleep you need, and be honest with yourself. Good sleep has so many benefits. I helped one of my girls set boundaries for herself to be able to fall asleep more easily. Some of my favorite tricks are turning out big or bright lights in the house when it starts getting dark outside and just using lamps or candles. Putting my phone on "do not disturb" and not watching TV in bed helps me. Listening to the Psalms on my Bible app or reading a book will quiet my mind to help me fall asleep. Taking a warm shower or spending a little extra time washing my face before bed also works. I love to use progressive muscle relaxation to help me sleep when my body is trying to stay awake. Starting at my toes and moving up to my face, I tense each muscle group and relax it slowly three times each. By the time I'm clenching my jaw and releasing tension, I'm yawning and half asleep. On nights I struggle more to relax my mind and my body is exhausted, free writing in a journal helps clear my head.

One of my girls introduced me to the practice of "sleep hygiene." It includes some of the things I mentioned before and as well as avoiding caffeine or food that disrupts sleep in the evenings, exercising regularly during the day, and creating a comfortable sleeping environment for yourself.

My bed is one of my favorite possessions. Over the years I have accumulated a king sized bed with a heated mattress pad. I have so many pillows and blankets that it's difficult to see me when I'm wrapped up in it all. I have an extensive collection of pajamas and house slippers on either side of my bed. If that's not your vibe, figure out what works for you to look forward to bed and start the process of transforming your sleep space. Then limit access to your bed as much as possible so that ideally it is used solely for sleep.

In setting a sleep schedule, getting out of bed right when I wake up in the morning helps. I don't set multiple alarms or snooze my first one. After 6am, unless I feel particularly inclined otherwise, I get out of bed as soon as my body naturally wakes up. This usually provides me with plenty of time to stretch, make tea, take a shower, and sit outside before I have to leave for work. Unintentional napping is the nemesis of my sleep routine. I experience more benefits going for a short walk or cleaning to regain energy than laying down and falling asleep in the middle of the day.

However, intentional naps can be miraculous life-giving activities. A nap and a snack is sometimes exactly what I need, so I try to be mindful of when napping is helpful to my energy levels and when it is harmful. Napping as a means of avoidance or emotional repression is a no-go. Napping from pure exhaustion or not sleeping the night before is a no-go. Napping past 4pm in this stage of life is a no-go. But napping to enjoy sleep and rest before re-engaging with my day is an easy yes.

Exercise: Exercise is an excellent life-giving activity. Whether you have time for a two-minute wall squat or an hour-long workout, prioritizing physical well-being is worth the effort. You can adapt your workouts to your lifestyle and your goals. In the summer when I'm out of work, I can work out for a couple of hours a day and still have time to go for a walk. During the school year, I'm happy to get in a ten minute stretching routine. For a while, I got into running on the treadmill, and later I enjoyed lifting weights more. Exercise serves you; you don't serve it. Make it what you like and what is best for your body. The more closely you align those two things, the more pleasant exercise will be for you.

My primary motivation in working out is reaching the endorphin high. It's been close to a drug for me since high school when I was heavily impacted by seasons of depression and generalized anxiety. The influence exercise has on mood is undeniable, and the people in your life will most likely find you much more pleasant when you're taking care of your body and getting those good chemicals.

Working out can also become an easy way to begin comparing yourself to others or hating yourself. That's a big no for life-giving rest. Celebrate your body, your small victories, and your efforts. We get one body and, whether you like it or not, it was intentionally created. Your body is wonderful, and you're the primary steward of it. Work toward your goals and cover yourself in grace. I feel more alive after a workout when I am thinking gracious thoughts toward myself and my progress than when I am judging myself or degrading my progress.

Healthy Eating: Eating healthy goes hand in hand with exercising. My diet typically improves when my exercise improves, and the inverse is true as well. One of my favorite memories with my grandmother was sitting in her kitchen and talking over apples and peanut butter. My go-to snack is rarely fruit and even less likely apples because I don't particularly enjoy them, but choosing to eat a "rare" healthy snack with my grandma was an impactful moment. My dad would sometimes slice up bananas and put them in the freezer as a healthy snack, so I started doing that in my own home. Even the process of slicing up a banana is restful and requires minimal effort. The few minutes it takes to prepare the snack are sometimes just enough to refuel me during my day. It's a baby break I get to take, and later I'll have a small reward of frozen banana slices for it.

Isolation: Isolation is a lot like napping when it comes to life-giving rest. If you need intentional alone time, you will be amazed at how restored you feel afterward. I am extraordinarily extroverted. I learned that I need to be social in order to relax sometimes. For the small percentage of me that is introverted, I need to isolate. Time alone can be a quick regeneration period to prepare for more social interaction. I have to be intentional not to abuse isolation to avoid someone or something. In those instances, isolation no longer serves as a tool of rest but a temporary band aid keeping me from dealing with necessary circumstances.

Hobbies: Hobbies are excellent life-giving activities and you can choose from endless options. I have tried my hand at a number of hobbies and moved on from them when I got bored. The purpose of hobbies isn't for me to become a master in a new skill but to experience what life has to offer. With that in mind, I don't feel pressured to have great results in what I pursue or to pursue the same thing for a long time. I've had hobbies like cooking, baking, volleyball, tennis, learning languages, painting, puzzles, guitar, and piano. I'm not great at any of these activities, but they have added to my array of experiences and enriched my life at times. Reading is one of my favorite hobbies. I pick things that interest me, like neuroscience or science fiction. I like to highlight my books and lend them to friends. I also find joy in going to a bookstore when I finish a book to pick out my next one, but maybe you'll find excitement roaming through the library or sifting through online reviews.

Routines: Getting in a routine is a way to guarantee life-giving rest has a piece of your time. Routines make sense to our bodies with our internal clocks; we function well when we abide by them. That's not to say we can't switch things up for some excitement or adapt our lifestyles for a better fit. However, we should have a structure to rely on as we construct our days. Daniel Simmons, a leader at the campus ministry I interned for, once told me that structure should bow to the mission. If the structure isn't the best for the intended purpose, then the structure should be bent or changed. I think we can live our lives in the same way. We set routines for ourselves to help us live well, but we can bend them a bit when they no longer serve the purpose. You are empowered to spend your time how you'd like to. You can choose when you rest and when you produce. You have the freedom to explore what works best for you.

I've come to find that most activities are neutral. Like Paul once said in 1 Corinthians (BSB), "Everything is permissible, but not everything is beneficial." We have to learn to use what we do for our benefit or choose not to do it. A social media platform where users share short videos was trending in my workplace for a while. Although I was often amused by my coworkers' re-enactments of videos, I didn't enjoy the social media platform. Instead of letting it eat up my time, I did other things I enjoyed to find rest. This social media not an inherently bad platform. One of my coworkers said it restored her faith in humanity because of it's humor. But I didn't need to pressure myself to buy into what's popular to feel like I belong. I can do whatever I want to do in the free time I create for myself, but I try to use wisdom to choose activities that are beneficial for me.

In Exodus 5, the Israelites, who had been enslaved by Egypt for hundreds of years, finally begin to ask for their freedom. Pharaoh increases their workload in response to Moses' request to release the Israelites. As I was reading this passage, I began to think about Pharaoh's solution. He may have believed that the dream of freedom was a product of too much time being idle. The chapter suggests that Pharaoh assumed their laziness and free time were contributing to their itch to live a different life. I think God encourages rest because when we relax, we can dream of a better life. Our imaginations are free to create different potential futures. God is not afraid of your ideas to walk in more freedom and a better life. Those are the plans that He has for you according to Jeremiah 29:11. Rest is an avenue for us to discover the potential that lies within us.

Promised Rest

Scripture is loaded with verses and stories about rest. When I struggle to rest, I remind myself that rest is a promise from God. It is a gift from Him; something I receive. I can partner with God in resting, but I don't have to generate it alone. In Matthew 11, Jesus says I can come to Him and He'll give me rest. In Psalm 4, David said he would lie down and sleep in peace because God makes him dwell in safety. Psalm 127 says that God grants sleep to those He loves. We miss out on a lot of things because we misunderstand or ignore what God has intended for us. Rest shouldn't have to be one of those things.

On the seventh day of the world's creation, God established the Sabbath—a day of rest He instructed His people to preserve each week. The beauty of the new covenant is that we have access to rest seven days a week through the comfort of the Spirit living in us. I protect at least an hour a day to rest. Though I am rarely successful, I aim to set aside a day each week to relieve myself from work. Responsibilities are dependable. They will still be piled up when I'm done taking time to refill. Sabbath is a time carved out to engage with the Holy Spirit. It's something I look forward to rather than something that feels like a waste of time.

Rest should be proactive. My life shouldn't consist of going from activity to activity draining myself and hoping I can make it to my next Sabbath moment. I should have a healthy balance between work and rest that provides the energy I need for each activity and space between activities to breathe. One of the ways I can do this is by protecting time to rest each week. I know I have a time to look forward to that nothing can infringe upon. Another way to cultivate rest is by taking intentional deep breaths throughout the day. These breaths are just brief moments when I can remind myself that I am a human and not a machine.

Intentionally choosing rest as a productive use of my time has greatly impacted the way that I work. Because I take time to rest, I have to manage my time better outside of those Sabbath moments, and my life is overall more productive. I have the energy emotionally and physically to meet the demands of each day. I have something to look forward to every day, even if my responsibilities seem dreary. This is a blessing from God I get to live in, and it's available to everyone.

On the days I can't manage a Sabbath moment or the day is unexpectedly interrupted, I take Jesus at His word that I can come to Him and He will give me rest. He is in every moment. Intentional moments with Him should not be replaced because He has offered constant help. The faithfulness of His promised rest serves as a trustworthy safety net beneath me. As I think of rest, I am reminded of the goodness of God. He is the peace of a calm day, the love in a restful moment, the Friend to unwind with when night falls. So often He is mistaken as a boss or a distant mystical being, but He is life and love. Knowing God in rest is one of the most beautiful, life-changing ways to know our Lord and Savior.

Resting with God protects me from striving for His acceptance or approval. It forces me to take a leap of faith that He loves me even when I am still. One of my favorite ways to rest with God is to be outside. I let my dog run around the backyard while I sit on my porch with a glass of water (or maybe a cup of tea if it's chilly outside). No music, no screens, no conversations. Just me, God, and the sounds of the world. To rest with God is to believe that you can let go of worry and pressure, without a crutch to distract you, and find peace. A "crutch" is anything we depend on in place of God. Drugs, sweets, alcohol, attention, projects, binge-watching, or even binge-reading are all crutches I've relied on or watched others rely on. Many other crutches exist because they can be anything. Notice what you turn to when you need rest and try to surrender that in place of pursuing genuine connection with God. Some things can be restful with God in certain seasons and in moderation. Some need to be surrendered entirely—particularly if an addiction has formed. A mentor, counselor, pastor, or godly friends can help you get off your crutches and into resting with God.

Challenge Yourself

I was reading a book on the calming effects of water when I came across the term "hedonistic habituation" for the first time. It refers to the fading degree of excitement we experience as we become accustomed to something that we enjoy. This particular book, Blue Mind, gave the example of living by the water. Author Wallace J. Nichols explains that people move by the water because they love the sound of the waves or watching the sunset over the water, but as the years pass by, the residents become less aware of the sound of the waves and less moved by the colors in the sunset. This habituation occurs with many activities and fascinations we chase. Fresh exposure to a person, place, or thing is a hefty component of the satisfaction we derive from whatever it is.

Part of rest is actually challenging yourself. It may seem counterintuitive, but a little challenge is the antidote to hedonistic habituation. Don't let yourself get bored with what you're doing. When you're around something too much, you get used to it. Switching things up and pushing yourself can increase the satisfaction you receive from how you're resting. Becoming passionless is no fun for anyone, and indifference does not contribute to a fulfilling life. Finding rest in God may look like embracing challenge.

Imagine you pick up tennis as a hobby. You love the sport, the adrenaline, the competition. But the more you play, the less exciting it is. There are high moments, but it's not as exciting as it was in the beginning. You get better and better, beating every competitor and begin to feel bored with the sport. Instead continuing to play despite your disinterest or dropping the sport altogether, you can join a stronger league. Push yourself, put yourself in a place where you might lose, and find the thrill of challenge.

Imagine you see someone across the room who is everything you've dreamed of and more. You make eye contact and approach one another. You get to know each other bit by bit and flirt. You feel butterflies and begin dating. You spend hours with the person then even more just thinking about the time you've spent together. Months into the relationship, you're comfortable and content, but it's nothing like the beginning. The newness has passed, and now you're just a part of each others' lives. You get married, and years into marriage, you find yourself basically coexisting with your partner. Occasionally you share a romantic moment, but you're both so familiar with each other that the spark has faded. This is the perfect opportunity to ask each other deeper questions, take a trip somewhere, try a new activity together, and pursue goals for your relationship.

Imagine you have a radical encounter with God and surrender your life to Jesus. Finally, life makes sense. You're full of hope and love. The people around you notice how your life has changed and how much happier you are. The freedom you are experiencing is unlike anything you've known before. You join a church and eagerly await each Sunday to grow in your faith and connect with other believers. Years into your walk with God, you find yourself reduced to praying before meals and only going to church because you committed to serving. Maybe you only go because your spouse really wants to, and you're relieved when you don't have to. In many ways, you feel like you have lost that first love you once had for Jesus.

You aren't the first. Jesus said the same thing to the Church in Ephesus (Revelation 2:4). Even when we've lost the feeling, Jesus is faithful. He promises a blessing to those who over-come—that they'd be able to eat of the tree of life in Paradise with God (Revelation 2:7). David prayed, "restore to me the joy of your salvation" in Psalm 51. When the initial excitement of our relationship with God wears off, we can have our joy re-stored. Press into your faith, whatever it takes, to find that pas-sion again you once knew.

Feeling settled and comfortable in certain seasons is accept-able and sometimes perfectly necessary. But life is more than the season we are in. You will find a time for everything: for the highs, the lows, and steadiness. Embrace the time you're in, but know you also have the ability to challenge yourself as a means of potentially shifting the way you're experiencing life. Some days I get really caught up watching movies alone in my room. While it's enjoyable, I know the best thing I could do for myself to get refilled after that is to get fresh air. Going for a walk, play-ing tennis with friends, and playing fetch with my dog are all physical activities that actually become a way for me to relax from the mind-fogging activity I was engaging in before. Rest needs to meet your mental, emotional, physical, social, and spiri-tual needs. You should never feel constrained in your ability to rest. There are few limitations to seeking refreshment; do what you need to do.

Loving Yourself
By cleaning up obstacles of hopelessness, limitation, and disruption with God, you've made more space for His love to fill more of you. Your life will get messy again– it never takes mine very long. Give yourself grace to hope anyway, mind your mind,

and accept the permission to be at peace. People who can live like that are the kind of people who make powerful leaders. They don't stop at knowing they are loved by God, they remain in the love of God and others begin to notice.

We are not in the light if we are not loving others. We won't see how to move forward in life and we won't be honoring God well. The love we receive has to flow beyond us, compelling us forward and leading others to God. To love others is not an obligation but a gift—a gift from God to you.

Part III: Loving Others
"By this the world will know you are My disciples, if you love one another." John 13:35

Unified

The Church consists of all who live according to the conviction that Jesus is Lord and God, and that He was raised from the dead after dying for the forgiveness of our sins (Romans 10; John 1). She, as we call her, is more all-encompassing than our home church or church away from home—she is the entire Body of Christ. She's the multi-cultural, beautiful Bride of Christ. I have big dreams for the Church and what she could be in this world. I love encouraging my girls to plug into local churches and hear about how they encounter God in the various services. I don't think attending church should have to be dull or forced.

When I hear people talking about only going to church a few times a year or having to drag their significant other to a service, it makes me sad. We miss out on incredible gifts from God when we skip church. Power and beauty hide inside a community of believers. My fascination with attending church is searching out and embracing those great qualities. I believe I'm an influencer in my church just by showing up and taking opportunities that are presented to me. I want my girls to see the value they offer to the churches they join and the value the churches have to offer them. It should be a mutual exchange of giving and receiving what we gain in God.

Her Purpose

I've seen the Church get so much criticism in America and the few places I've traveled to in Europe. We're hypocrites, we're idiots, we're judgmental. We've hurt people, we're the blind leading the blind—I've heard it all. I have been heavily involved in several ministries, and I haven't been a part of a single one that was perfectly pure and righteous.

Sometimes, the deeper you get involved with a ministry, the more you see how broken the ministers truly are. Then you can look across ministries and see how much disunity exists. Denominations, theological debates, competition, snide remarks, and blatant offensive statements have all been a part of American Church culture. Tragedies have happened at the hands of priests, and horrific events have taken place that were ignored by pastors for insufficient reasons. It's no wonder that people don't want to be a part of the Church. Two things I know:

God loves the Church.

God has called us to love the Church.

We, the Church, are the city on the hill. We are salt and light (Matthew 5). We are called to be different from the rest of the wounded world (1 Peter 2). Following Christ should transform our lives. Our holiness, our "set-apart-ness," should be visible to the rest of the world. I think it's similar to what Paul meant when he spoke about the Gentiles provoking the Israelites to jealousy as they entered salvation (Romans 11). The world should see us and want what we have. I don't think that's going to happen if we don't change the way we see the Church.

If you've ever been to church, you've probably been hurt by someone in the church or disagreed with a church leader at some point. I'd encourage you to let God heal that wound, so He can restore you back to the Body. He created you to coexist with other believers, despite how difficult that may seem at times. Bitterness is doing nothing for you and, honestly, I think forgiveness is more your color. In light of all of her many flaws, luckily, we've been given God-approved advice on restoring, healing, purifying, and beautifying His Church to the fullness of unity in the image of Christ, without blemish or wrinkle. I've got a few practical thoughts as well, but I want to provide vision first.

The Church is the Bride of Christ. She is who Jesus died for, the joy set before Him, the pearl of great price, the reward of His suffering, and His inheritance. That's a big deal. God has never referred to the Church as insignificant or hopeless. He really cares about it, and He deeply desires her. He wants the Church to be blameless and walking worthy of her calling (1 Thessalonians 5:23). The Bride of Christ has influence through her relationship with Christ and should confidently function in His authority.

Our first hurdle is understanding who the Church is. If you are in Christ, you are part of the Church. Now you can see how hating the Church is just another seed of self-hatred you have growing in your garden. Uproot that, and let God change your perspective with truth. You're part of the family now, part of the Body. And the Body includes all believers in Christ throughout the world, not just the people you respect, admire, and have great relationships with. This means if your ex-husband, the pastor who hurt you, the man who took advantage of you, your friend who betrayed you, are following God, they're part of the Church too. That could sound like incredibly bad news to some.

Figure out how to establish healthy boundaries and walk in forgiveness. The best you can do is to love. It's not always going to be easy, but it is possible because Jesus made a way. Loving people who have hurt you will take a literal miracle and will most likely be entirely undeserved. In God you have that power. How that translates in your daily life is between you and the Lord (and maybe a trusted advisor), but it's worth pursuing. When I feel stuck in a moment and don't know how to love someone, I ask God for just one thing I can do or say that would honor Him. I also talk to leaders in my life about how to interact with people I struggle to love well and when to take a step back from a difficult relationship. You'll find answers as you search for them in wise counsel.

Inside or outside of churches, be intentional with what you do or don't do. Leaders are absolutely going to let you down because leading is hard. Under all their confidence and influence are human beings who only know what they know. If you don't speak up for yourself or you dedicate time doing things for them, you might walk away feeling abused, used, and taken advantage of. But if you're intentional then when you speak up you can live with the peace of having said your part. When you do things for them, you can serve with willingness and purpose. When leaders let you down, it's not necessarily that they're bad leaders. It's likely that they're not much further along than you are in some ways. You're not alone in your disappointment. But choose to give leaders grace and to trust them anyway if you believe in the destination they're trying to get you to. Finding a balance between holding to your values and trusting leadership is key. The Holy Spirit will help you.

The Church is more than the church you attend or your denomination. It's more than the Church in America. The Church is beautifully diverse and extends all over creation. I feel strong personal conviction that we should celebrate the various ways people engage with God. Explore what Christianity looks like around the globe. Adapt your faith to things you like and acknowledge the good God has placed in practices you don't want to adopt as your own. There's no reason to be close-minded about different traditions or expressions of faith. If it edifies someone to read liturgy, don't let yourself check out mentally from what God could be doing in that moment. If it increases someone's faith to wave flags and dance during worship, don't let that distract you from connection with God and the Body of Christ.

We all interact with God uniquely because we were each created uniquely. We can share ideas, songs, theologies, and make earth look a little more like Heaven. A friend of mine once said, "Your preferences aren't always important." That stuck with me for weeks as I thought about how much I miss out on in life because I only do what I want to do or what feels comfortable. The Church is just a bunch of people who wanted to be loved. I don't have to make it about me all the time. I have the grace in God to take care of me and take care of those around me. My capacity to minister increases as I choose humility.

When it comes to churches or people I disagree with, I've chosen to engage. You can learn anything from anyone, even if you don't like their stance or perspective. You don't have to throw out the baby with the bathwater. Engaging with someone when we don't see eye to eye challenges us to grow, learn, and stretch. It may be uncomfortable, but interacting in humility while keeping your focus on God is fun. You'll see God do things you don't normally see Him do or hear Him say things you wouldn't normally hear in your usual circles. You'll witness people facing different kinds of difficulties than your own and, thus, witness different kinds of miracles. This doesn't mean you should tolerate false doctrine or submit yourself to questionable leadership. You don't have to commit to a church you disagree with. I don't feel pressure to intentionally reach out to people I don't enjoy ministering with or to attend church where I don't feel called, but I also don't feel an instinct to turn away from those people and places if they reach out to me.

One of the most empowering tools I've found in situations where I disagree is to communicate respectfully. The stakes usually aren't as high as we place them. I think if we were all meant to agree, God would have made us know everything like He does. He could have, but He didn't. Having conversations with others, even if you don't hold the same views as each other, is an avenue for building relationships. It's valuable to talk with people who are different than you. Develop compassion for other perspectives and challenge your thinking. Don't debate; converse. A healthy communicative relationship with another person will rarely come back to bite. We don't have to be like the people around us to be like Jesus. Luke was a doctor, Peter a fisherman, and Matthew a tax collector. I'm sure they could have found things to disagree on and bicker about. We see the disciples argue plenty throughout the Gospels, but that never stopped them from following Jesus together.

When my parents divorced, my mom moved and started attending a new church. I had already been hearing negative comments about my home church from others, and in the chaos of the divorce, I had to think for the first time about whether or not to take them seriously. I was seeing a therapist to help process life, and she encouraged me to look for fruit. A good tree produces good fruit. If I could see God moving in a church, see Him blessing people, and hear the truth being preached, then I could honor the church because of what God was doing there. I didn't have to choose sides anymore. I could appreciate the positive impact the church had made on my life but still go where I felt God leading me.

As I matured in faith, I found extraordinary comfort in personal conviction. God had established my dad in one church and established my mom in another. God gave me two choices: to follow Him or follow where pressure in conflict was leading me. I chose the former. I didn't have to pick a parent or a church, I got to follow God. Now, as an adult, I feel confident in my ability to follow personal conviction from God. I know that He speaks to me and that I hear Him. We've had years of building a relationship in which He leads me into good things, and I trust Him to lead me.

If you are struggling with which church to attend, ask God

where He's calling you. Then look at the fruit of that ministry. What are its core values and mission statement? Does that align with what God has put on your heart? Where can it be pruned or strengthened? Do you feel grace toward its weaknesses? You not only have power to choose, you have power to change. You are a revivalist wherever you go because Christ is in you. Find a home church, and make it what you want it to be. This doesn't mean you conform the church to your preferences, but that you engage with the church in ways that build it up. You don't need a platform to change your environment or to usurp the authority of the leaders who God established in the church. Start small, communicate ideas, ask for help. You can be a catalyst for redemption in your church. You're not powerless, no matter what title you lack or position you don't fill. In being part of a church and living by the Spirit, you are producing good fruit there which should draw people in.

One of my friends was struggling to choose which church to attend because her parents had strong opinions on the matter. They, like many well-intended parents, were concerned their daughter would join a church that didn't offer the "meat and bones" of Scripture. Many "seeker-sensitive" churches exist in the States, but that doesn't disqualify them from being a church that you can grow in even if you've been saved for decades. As long as the legitimate Gospel of Jesus is being preached, you can learn.

Maturing in faith is training yourself to know good from evil (Hebrews 5:14). You're no longer relying on a pastor or preaching to give you truth; you can find it yourself. So wherever you're attending church, whether they preach the love of God or eschatology, you can take it to God and ask what He has to teach you through the message. He will lead you into all truth (John 16:13). Talk to Him about what you're hearing and study the Scriptures for yourself.

We don't know everything. There's so much division in beliefs and theology. Sometimes you just have to take a leap of faith into what you think God is calling you to because there's so much we don't know. We try our best, and we embrace the grace extended to us in our failures. Some things are explicitly right, some are explicitly wrong. Jesus is the only way to the Father— explicitly right. Hell does not exist—explicitly wrong. Our measure for truth is the Bible.

Still, gray areas exist that the Spirit must lead us through. We should learn to extend grace to those around us in place of exalting ourselves in pride. We should trust the conviction of the Spirit and the inspiration of Scripture while also recognizing that our interpretations of Scripture can put us at odds with one another. A common disagreement in the Church is related to baptism. Can you be baptized multiple times or once? Should you be sprinkled or immersed? Your interpretation of Scripture can lead you to a conclusion entirely plausible and yet entirely different from someone else's.

Believing Jesus died for our sins and was raised from the dead is a non-negotiable. The Gospels and the Epistles are clear that this is true and necessary to believe in order to receive salvation. But it's not about knowing enough to pass a test to get into heaven. This is about immersing ourselves in the love of God through pursuing knowledge and understanding of His truth, and living in relationship with God forever.

I heard a message by Bob Sorge my first year out of college. He said he attends church every week just to be able to say that he was standing there on his own two feet. He wasn't going to miss out if God was going to move on a Sunday morning where believers are gathered together. He wasn't going to be absent for a message or testimony particularly breathed on by God. His resolve to be engaged with a church was inspiring.

I went church-fishing through all of college and the following year. Traveling got in the way of regularly attending a church, but the most honest answer was that I didn't particularly enjoy church. I didn't enjoy waking up early enough Sunday morning to get dressed up to see a bunch of people I don't know and sing songs I can sing at home and listen to a sermon on a verse I could read at home. I was often bored in services and always hungry for lunch. My inner critic was nearly impossible to turn off—when it wasn't questioning the biblical accuracy of the pastor's message, it was judging outfits, Southern accents, and expressions of worship.

I was intrigued one day by the purpose of attending church. Reflecting on Acts and Paul's letters, I began to notice the early Church was wild. They argued over each other both in services and outside of them, spoke in tongues whenever they felt like it without explanation, dressed like the highly-sexualized culture around them, and all kinds of crazy in many places. In all that mess, I'm reminded of one of my favorite passages in Scripture: 1 Corinthians 12-14.

Paul gave instructions to establish order and purpose into the Church that so desperately needed, and still desperately needs, wisdom. He teaches them about spiritual gifts that we see listed out here and in a few other places in Scripture. He shares that we have all been given gifts from the same Spirit for the common good exactly as God intends. He also encourages us to eagerly to eagerly desire more spiritual gifts. He explains how God created the Church to be both diverse yet unified. Paul then acknowledges the differences we possess that cause disunity, and in light of that, He shares 1 Corinthians 13 as the solution. Essentially, whatever we do is pointless without love. We are nothing and we gain nothing if we don't have the qualities of love evident in all of it. Qualities of love include kindness and humility but also rejoicing in truth and not delighting in evil. So as we focus on love, we don't want to throw caution to the wind.

In chapter 14, it gets really good. Paul advises the Church to excel in the gifts that build up the Church. Over and over again, he highlights the importance of strengthening the Church. Church shouldn't just be an individual experience, it should be a community of people actively encountering God through relationships with one another. That's what I was missing out on my church experience. I was attending as if it were only for my good. My involvement in church is actually for the edification of the Church, through which I am edified, and not for my own selfish gain.

Like the people referred to in Hebrews 5, I was going to church to "drink milk" or "glean spiritual nourishment" from someone else. It's no wonder I was unsatisfied leaving the service. Desiring growth in my relationship with God, I was craving meat but expecting it from pastors and leaders rather than seeking it from God directly. God does have solid food for us in church. We must be willing to give ourselves to both seeking the Scriptures ourselves and being willing to share what we learn with others in order to taste the meat. We must be willing to mature in our faith, receiving meat from God and giving it away.

Maturing in faith means I should be able to go in and teach, but I don't have to. Again, leadership doesn't need a platform. I can lead in my church by faithfully attending, by volunteering, and by creating ministry opportunities in the community. My friend Scottlyn is an exceptional example of this. She greets me every Sunday at church and we sit together. For a couple months, I would pick up Starbucks for us on her bill and sit with her while she worked at the church after the services. Watching her work brought healing to my experience of church because she served with humility and kindness. As she walked the halls, she greeted the people we passed by name. She didn't worship-lead, give the announcements, or preach sermons. She loved people well and served with the gifts she had.

I think God created us to freely receive and to freely give abundant life. Because of that, I believe I will have a more life-giving experience in church when I'm building up others and being built up. Which leads me to one of the most important discoveries I've learned about the Church: it was meant to unite us in real relationships.

Pretty obvious, I now know. Church is so much more fun when you feel connected and a sense of belonging from knowing the people around you well. I think every church I've ever attended has had opportunities for deeper involvement. Even if it didn't, I could turn to the person next to me and invite them out to coffee or lunch. We act like social scripts restrict us from creating relationships with the members of our own Body and, in doing so, we forget the purpose of church is unity with God and one another. Christian community has perks that you can't find anywhere else. These people are commanded—by God—to love you. That's a pretty sweet deal. They may not always live up to it, but then we have an amazing gift called mercy that leads to restoration and strengthening of relationships.

Many churches provide opportunities to connect with mentors who will give you wisdom you never knew you needed. My discipler, Kimberly, has completely transformed the way I process my emotions. I used to be ashamed of being sad, but now I embrace sadness (with significantly less resistance) as a way to make more room for the Holy Spirit.

Churches can also provide opportunities for discipling younger people. Mentoring younger women can help redeem the painful parts of your story by helping someone walk through similar struggles toward hope. My girls have heard about some of my dumbest mistakes but can learn from what I've done to avoid making those mistakes in the future. I can't change my past, but I can offer wisdom from my experiences to help them protect their futures from similar shortcomings.

Church relationships emulate iron sharpening iron—friend-ships that challenge you to live a standard of excellence drowned in grace. Sometimes I think I'm living in freedom, like I'm doing the best I can and thriving. Then I look at the freedom my friends in the Church have and realize there's so much more available for me.

Church communities also offer deep care for one another. When I came back to town after weeks of being involved in a family emergency, my friends Tori and Emily met me at my favorite chocolate shop with a couple of frozen dinners, flowers, and a card. I felt seen and cared for by them. While relationships can be petty, careless, dramatic, and troublesome, they can also be beautiful. Community is so messy, but it's even more worth it. All it takes is showing up and following that personal conviction of how to love others best in every situation. The Holy Spirit is dwelling inside you and giving you everything you need to change what you've known the Church to be.

If you don't experience the Holy Spirit in church, that's between you and God. Don't blame disconnects between you and God on the Church or leaders in a service. God wants to connect with you through feelings, ideas, conversations, teachings, worship, sensations, and probably many other ways I'm not even aware of. The environment of some churches you attend may not be your preference, but that doesn't keep the Spirit of God out. You bring the Holy Spirit with you wherever you go because He dwells in you. And don't forget the Holy Spirit can look unfamiliar to you at times. He may be doing something in a pastor or congregation you've never seen before. Don't miss out on knowing more of God because the Church doesn't look like you think it should. The Church isn't supposed to look like you—it's supposed to look like God.

Different ministries are like different worship songs. They have individual purposes and messages, but they're all meant to glorify God. They can work together to unify the Body even though they have unique qualities. Find the way you connect with God, whether that's through your church, a church you visit, a family you attend dinner with, or wherever else you love people in alignment with the truth of Scripture.

Don't limit Him to a building—find Him in every building. I don't think connecting with God outside of church means you don't need to go to church anymore. I don't think noticing God's presence in a bar means you should go out every weekend. But I think we limit God when we try to confine Him to a service. We are the body of Christ meant to glorify the Father. We don't need to forfeit our identities as the Church because of our prejudices. Christ died to set us free from that, to empower us for more than that.

The world needs the Church. I remember being moved to tears hearing the testimony of a woman who survived the Hundred Days of Slaughter during the 1994 genocide in Rwanda. Her words cut to my core as she recited the tragedy she endured. "Where was God in the hundred days of genocide?" she asked the audience. Responding to her own question before we could wonder, she said, "No, where was the Church?"

God was there in her pain. God was with her as her family was being murdered in the next room over, and her people were falling one by one throughout the streets. She resolved in those horrific moments to strengthen the Church if God preserved her life through the devastation. Her conviction was to teach the Church to trust God.

I wish the Church would have responded better or aided in preventative measures so things might have been different during those hundred days in Rwanda. But that's not the only travesty the world has endured while the Church stayed within it's four walls. Both on individual and global levels, the Church has fallen short because we aren't responding with the authority Christ died to give us. Equal to urgency, we should feel the immense possibility. We have been given responsibility and unparalleled opportunity to save, heal, and deliver the world. Open your eyes and see the world through the lens of the God who so loved the world that He gave His one and only son. Whoever believes in the Gospel you have inside you won't perish but have eternal life. Open your mouth and see a world changed.

Audrey Hepburn once said, "You may be one person to the world, but you may also be the world to one person." You should be the person who changes someone's whole world. There's that much power inside you. It's hidden in your compassion, your encouragement, your finances, your hospitality, your evangelism, and so many other aspects of your life. You are the Church, and we need you to be you.

Spiritual Gifts

Gifts from the Spirit are one of the aspects of my faith that consistently bring joy. I think that's part of their purpose because we know a fruit of the Spirit is joy (Galatians 5:22-23). It makes sense that gifts from Him would produce that fruit. I was blessed to grow up with spiritual gifts as a normal part of how I understood and expressed my faith. I had leaders I could learn from and who supported me as I grew in the giftings God had given me. I was eager to receive gifts from God, even if those gifts seemed strange to other people. I was fascinated by the Bible and able to discover much about the gifts of the Spirit from my personal time in the Word. I think Christians sometimes avoid conversations about spiritual gifts because there's intimidation and confusion swirling around charismatic expressions of faith, but every good and perfect gift is from God. Nothing should keep us from receiving that.

The majority of my foundation in Scripture for spiritual gifts comes from 1 Corinthians 12-14. If you were to look in my Bible I bought a few years ago, you'd find these three chapters highlighted, underlined, and written around. I'm undecided as to whether it's more beautiful that way or just more chaotic. I see churches functioning in the gifts the same way sometimes.

In these chapters, Paul is addressing the Church in Corinth quite directly to give guidance where believers are passionately functioning in the gifts. The context clues for this begin in verse 1 of chapter 12 when he says, "Now about the gifts of the Spirit, brothers and sisters, I do not want you to be uninformed." To me this indicates that the gifts are something the early church was familiar with and also something the Church should know about today. Because it was canonized, I also assume it's God-breathed and pertaining to the Church.

Paul teaches a few main concepts to educate the Church on the gifts: every gift comes from the Holy Spirit (1 Corinthians 12:4), every gift brings glory to God (1 Corinthians 12:6), and every gift is meant to strengthen the Church (1 Corinthians 12:7). Paul lists various spiritual gifts in 1 Corinthians and Ephesians, and other gifts are also documented outside of what Paul mentioned, leading us to believe his lists are not exhaustive. He finishes chapter 12 by encouraging everyone to eagerly desire the gifts—especially the gift of prophecy. This is an instruction that we often overlook but even more-so an invitation for our own pleasure and excitement. Think about Christmas or birthdays. Looking forward to gifts is part of the joy of the celebration. Part of our daily walk with God is to live like it's almost a holiday all the time.

Here's a non-extensive overview of some of the gifts Paul lists that the Holy Spirit gives:

Wisdom: I've seen the gift of wisdom operate in a number of my girls. They describe hearing themselves share thoughts or ideas beyond their natural intellectual capabilities and knowing the gift of wisdom must have been at work. They experience an enlightened moment that provides an unparalleled solution. Wisdom is highly esteemed in Scripture, especially Proverbs. Even Paul prays that the Church in Ephesus would receive the Spirit of wisdom. To desire this gift is to desire understanding that is in alignment with truth.

Knowledge: I've both witnessed and experienced the gift of knowledge many times in ministry. Those are the strange moments in which a person just knows something all of the sudden about a person, place, or thing that only God could have revealed to them. Jack Deere came to speak at a ministry I worked at and toward the end of his teaching, he said, "I think someone in here has trouble hearing. She's sitting in this particular area and should come up to receive prayer for healing." A girl got up, received prayer for healing, and was able to hear out of her mostly-deafened ear again. The next night, she opened our service with the testimony of what God had done. Jack Deere "guessing" that someone needed healing for hearing was the gift of knowledge. He most likely felt a slight impression from God that he acted on or maybe felt a sensation in his ears that clued him into what God wanted to do. To desire this gift is to desire knowing things only God could know for the sake of revealing His love to others.

Faith: One of my friends has a significant gift of faith. More than the intense optimism that I carry, she has nearly unwavering belief in God and what He can do. This inner strength encourages people around her and sustains her through her struggles in life. She's not one to back down. She'll take God at His word and often see miracles because she doesn't give up. To desire this gift is to desire a supernatural conviction and assurance that God is who He says He is.

Healing: I took a trip out to a ministry known in part for its gift of healing. My coworker loved running but couldn't run comfortably because her hips were uneven due to one leg being longer than the other. We were listening to a teaching on healing when the leader invited people who wanted healing to receive prayer. My coworker raised her hand, and the leader prayed for her. Her leg grew out two inches, and she was able to run without pain from that day on. It was incredible. While I am so thankful for her healing, many people we prayed for didn't get healed at that moment. I can't say why healing happens sometimes and why it doesn't during others, why some people get healed and why others don't. But I do know God is still giving this gift to His Church today. To desire this gift is to desire releasing Jesus' healing power into hurting people.

Miracles: One of my friends has a contentious relationship with her parents at best. But one afternoon, she had a conversation that shifted the dynamics of their relationship. She was telling me how strange it was that, all the sudden, they could communicate effectively with each other and respect one another. That was a miracle. It was impossible apart from the power of God. Before that moment, nothing in their interactions would have predicted a turn toward relational health. But the Holy Spirit intervened and brought peace. The gift of miracles is that and more. I think healing is a miracle. I think Peter walking on water and Philip traveling in the Spirit were miracles. To desire this gift is to desire impossibilities becoming possible by the power of God.

Prophecy: A trusted leader told me he believed I would be a "champion of other champions." He felt that I would be able to identify influential people and encourage them in their potential. I was encouraged. A couple months later, I left the country and met with a leader in the UK who has the gift of prophecy. He didn't know anything about me other than my name, but as he prayed for me, he said to God, "I believe You have made her a leader of leaders." My friends who had heard the leader back home tell me the same sentiment all gasped. I began to cry, feel-

117

ing so deeply known by God. I had strengthened trust in His purpose for my life. To desire the gift of prophecy is to desire hearing what God has to say to a person and relaying the message in love.

Discernment: One of my girls told me that she met someone and all of the sudden just knew that the person she met was significant. She felt like the girl was trustworthy. She was discerning a spirit of goodness in this girl that allowed her to build a friendship. Another friend of mine was having a good day but walked into a room and immediately felt depressed. Nothing had changed that would have caused this emotional twist, so she asked God to show her what was going on. She discovered she was discerning a spirit of depression in the room. She later got to pray for a girl who struggled with depression to receive peace and love. She felt like God had made her aware of the heaviness of depression so that she could help people out of depressive states. Discernment is the distinguishing of spirits. To desire this gift is to desire sensing spiritual influences so that you can pray for God's Spirit to enhance what He is doing and redeem what is not His will.

Tongues: Since I was a kid, I've imagined tongues to be my secret language with God that the devil cannot decipher. As I've grown, I've learned tongues edifies my own spirit in the way receiving prophecy edifies my spirit. Some of my friends will find themselves speaking in tongues when they feel the Holy Spirit more apparently than other times. Others will be praying and a word will come to mind that they don't recognize. When they look it up, it usually translates from another language into something they can pray in their native tongue. To desire this gift is to desire strengthening your intimacy with God by verbally expressing faith in words previously unknown to you.

Interpretation of Tongues: When the gift of tongues is used in a corporate setting, interpretation of tongues is the gift God has given to bring unity. Paul explains that the gift of tongues is a sign to unbelievers (1 Corinthians 14). He also says that if unbelievers witness it, they will probably think we are out of our minds. Interpretation of tongues is receiving a translation of what has been spoken to bring clarity of what God is saying for all who are listening. To desire this gift is to desire boldness and supernatural understanding of languages known and unknown.

Beautiful Gifts

Paul instructs us to function in the gifts in the most excellent way. We want to receive gifts God has generously given to us and use them well. They are meant to bring glory to God and encourage each other. I'm personally inclined to pursue the most excellent way, so I continue reading to 1 Corinthians 13 in which I learn all the gifts are best complemented by love. All the gifts are actually less meaningful if they aren't used to spread God's perfect love.

Receiving a gift from someone who is distant or disengaged is awkward at best and hurtful in worse cases. Imagine the dad who works and travels all the time, never checking in with family and always exhausted when he's home. He gives out of a sense of responsibility, maybe a desperate attempt for reconnection, or maybe from the self-validation of affirming his own attempts at parenthood. The child receiving a gift from that father will likely not feel moved or blessed by the sentiment. Love is what brings meaning to the gifts.

In the same way, it would be difficult for me to receive a prophetic word from a leader who is using me or habitually walking over me. Though he may really be hearing from God and sharing His words with me, if we do not have an avenue of love through which I can trust him, I may struggle to receive what God is sharing through him. Another example is the stereotypical revivalist who has become power-hungry rather than sustained by love. He pushes people over while he lays a hand on their heads in prayer so it looks like the Spirit is moving. Those people are more likely to receive a bruised hip than the love of God through that kind of man.

Love doesn't necessarily imply relationship—at least not a long-term relationship. I've been able to minister to hundreds of students who come up to the altar after a service in need of prayer and encouragement. I can love each one of them. I can ask their names, ask what they want prayer for, share what I feel like God is saying, and even give them a hug before they walk away. Those are some of the moments I get to partner with God in transforming lives through the power of love sustaining the gifts of the Spirit.

Toward the end of chapter 13, Paul creates space for mistakes. He basically tells us that we are immature and don't know everything. But we have the hope that one day we will. We can mess up as long as we're motivated by love because love never fails, it always remains, and it's our greatest strength. The boundary for spiritual gifts is love. The source of spiritual gifts is love. The avenue for spiritual gifts is love. Love covers our shortcomings and lack of knowledge. If you have love, you have it all—even when you make a mistake. If you don't have love, your gifts are of no value.

My encouragement to those who are more charismatic is to love well. If the person you're using spiritual gifts for doesn't feel loved and walk away knowing they are deeply loved, you really missed the point. It's not about you. It's about God being glorified through a revelation of His love. I like to be intentional with each person I use spiritual gifts around to ask how they feel at the end. If I help them with something, I ask if I can do anything else. If I prophesy over someone, I ask if they feel encouraged. If I give someone wisdom, I ask if it was relevant. And I'm okay when I'm wrong because my goal isn't to be perfect at a gift, it's to love them. Having a conversation about how it made them feel gives them the space to reject me, but it also creates an opportunity for me to love them like they want to be loved.

My encouragement to those who are on the more conservative side, especially to my cessationist friends, is to eagerly desire these gifts as a part of your journey to know God's love more. When I was at a house church in Scotland, I met a young woman whose father was a cessationist theologian. I had no idea she was a cessationist until after I had let our leadership team loose to prophesy over anyone in the room they felt led to for twenty minutes. I encouraged anyone who was a part of the house church to come talk to me if they wanted to at the end.

Luckily for me, the young woman approached me and we had an amazing conversation. Her beliefs that the Holy Spirit doesn't release gifts anymore were nothing out of the ordinary. Her father had raised her to believe that the gifts of the Spirit were meant to authenticate Scripture and the authority of the original apostles, but we don't need them or see them anymore. Neither of us had intentions to argue with one another. She was mostly intrigued by the prophecy she had just witnessed first hand.

I encouraged her to ask the Holy Spirit for a fresh perspective as she read through the Bible, especially 1 Corinthians 12-14. For what might have been the first time in her life, she was excited to learn about spiritual gifts. I couldn't ask her to abandon her beliefs and her father's studies to blindly accept what I said based on some unusual ministry time. I wanted her to learn more about God through His gracious, supernatural gifts. I wanted her to hear from the Holy Spirit as she prayed about the gifts. I wanted her to open up the same Bible she had read hundreds of times and see something new. I was excited for her to find out God is even more fun and generous than she thought He was.

Spiritual gifts are fun; they are a part of living an abundant life with the Holy Spirit in us. They are for anyone in Christ to build up the Church, make us more like Christ, bring the Kingdom to earth, and glorify God. Wisdom did not cease when the original apostles died, nor hospitality, so why should we explain away other gifts?

I was a part of a ministry for four years that taught students about the gifts of prophecy, healing, and evangelism. Growing up, my environment encouraged prophecy and made space for it to be safely practiced. Enlightening college students about what the gift of prophecy is and how to function in that gift became one of my favorite parts of my job when I grew older. The students were eager to learn and full of questions. Prophecy occurs all throughout the Old Testament, and we even see entire books devoted to the prophecies of certain prophets. Jesus came and fulfilled those prophecies, but we see prophecy continues on in the New Testament. Paul instructs the Church to pursue all the spiritual gifts, especially prophecy. And even in Revelation we see that prophets are raised up in the future. Eventually prophecy will be done away with because we'll all be face to face with God, but my understanding of Scripture leads me to believe it's available for now (1 Corinthians 13:8).

Prophets of the Old Testament were messengers who heard from God and shared His words with others. I believe those with the gift of prophecy under the New Covenant serve the same purpose but with a twist because now anyone in Christ can hear from God. If you couldn't, you wouldn't be saved. He revealed Himself to you, called you to Himself, and loved you first. You responded to His voice. So when we prophesy, we prophesy in partial knowledge. We don't know anything for certain other than that which God has established in Scripture. But we can encourage each other with what we believe we hear God say and let the people we minister to decide if it's relevant.

In receiving a prophetic word, our job is to test it. We can ask God if that message was what He wanted to communicate to us. We can compare it to the Bible to make sure it doesn't contradict any truth revealed in Scripture. We can share it with trusted friends and leaders to figure out how to apply it to our lives. Just because someone says they have a prophetic word for you doesn't mean that word is true, is from God, was communicated effectively, or that you have to believe it. The person delivering the prophetic word is responsible to share it in love; you are responsible to test the word with the Word and talk to God about how He would like you to apply that word (if it was from Him). The most important guideline for new covenant prophecy is love. If a word is not given in love, it's garbage. Don't say it without love. Prophecy, like every gift, is given by Love to love on the Church by a loving beloved of Love. If you use the gift as it's intended, it shouldn't produce division, hopelessness, or insecurity.

All the gifts are worth nothing apart from love. Christmas morning is just a party of entitlement, greed, and inevitable emptiness without the bond of connection. Gifts don't distract from the loving giver; they are a blessing flowing from a deeper relationship. They are a celebration of being known and knowing someone in return. If the Holy Spirit didn't want us to have them and use them, I don't think He'd give them to us. People will fake using spiritual gifts for glory or validation; don't be like those people. Be a child convinced of the love of the Father and cheerfully willing to generously share that love with others.

Women in the Church

The Bible has a few verses that appear to be oppressive toward women. My girls who have happened upon them always have questions. So do I. My father is amazing and has been one of the leaders in my life to explain the context of those verses and the overall truth of the Word. He taught me that my interpretation of Scripture verses has to be consistent with the whole of Scripture. Great advice. One of the verses that I keep coming back to is Galatians 3:28-29, "There is neither Jew nor Gentile, neither slave nor free, nor is there male and female, for you are all one in Christ. If you belong to Christ, then you are Abraham's seed and heirs according to the promise."

In this verse, equality is brought to all people, regardless of ethnicity, status, or sex. In Christ, we are all heirs to the Kingdom. My dad challenged me to consider what we should do with women like Deborah and Miriam if God intends for women to be led and not to lead? What do we do with prophetesses like Anna and Huldah if God intends for women to listen and not to speak? What do we do with Priscilla if women shouldn't be over churches and should never instruct men? Ephesians 5 says, "be filled with the Spirit... submitting to one another out of reverence for Christ."

Mutual submission indicates a power balance and equitable division of responsibility. Sex-based oppression shouldn't be a part of the Church body. God said it was not good for man to be alone, so he made women fit for men. Not to help cook and clean but to have dominion over the earth, to be fruitful, to display the image of God. I believe women are not the stepping stones on whom men achieve their ultimate callings but co-heirs with Christ and with their brothers in the faith.

Restoring a power imbalance to equilibrium is no easy undertaking. It is one of therapy's most difficult problems examined; it falls in the category of damaging problems along with addiction, abuse, and extramarital affairs, according to my college course on intimate relationships. The severity of imbalance between genders in the Church is worth our concern, at the very least. Power is having control over a valuable resource. What valuable resources from God are extended to men and withheld from women? We are all heirs as children of God.

Social sciences have discovered that shared power in relationships is more beneficial because sustained energy over time requires equitable division of power. I imagine God designed relationships to profit with power balance because He likes for men and women to work together, which aligns with overarching themes of Scripture. The few verses suggesting inequality should be weighed against those themes.

My last thought I'll say on the subject is this: in Jesus' full submission to the Father, He taught, healed, led, prophesied, and served. What if unity in the Church was meant to reflect the unity of the Trinity and submission was never meant to restrict but to encourage one another into our Spirit-led purposes?

How you choose to interpret Scripture is between you and God. Some passages will be easier to understand than others. In your consideration of the more difficult verses, I implore you to remember the character of God and the narrative of the entire Bible. Let those be the lenses through which you decipher the mysteries. We don't know everything, but we do know there is truth at the end of every string we pull in the Word. We don't even necessarily need to know the answers to the question of women's roles in the Church if we don't want to. But if you have been made to feel insignificant or hushed because of your sex, you deserve to know that you are valued, you are significant, and you are empowered, both in and out of traditional roles.

Empowered

Empowerment is receiving authority and gaining confidence to do something. I became passionate about living an empowered life when my discipler first unveiled to me a world in which I matter. Through her consistency, wisdom, and care, she taught me that I was worth investing in. As a result, I began to understand that living as a child of God means more than I had imagined. I had thought I would grow from a good Christian girl into a good Christian woman, spending every day praying and loving Jesus. That's still true and still amazing.

But when she revealed the truth about the power Jesus gave me when I received His Spirit, I began to dream about my life with an even greater hope and imagination. Being a child of God means I have influence in my life and in the world around me. I can take the elements around me and create beauty. I am not enslaved to anyone or anything anymore. I'm free.

I want my girls to embrace the authority they've received in their adoption by God because they matter. They are world-changers in significant ways, whether their impacts redeem their families or echo through nations. This power is available to each one of them and for all who believe in Christ. He made it possible for all of us. Undoubtedly, the goodness of God leads us into empowered lives.

The Victim Mindset

One of the greatest barriers to empowerment that I've seen is a victim mindset—a schema that convinces people the world is out to get them, they are helpless, or they have been wronged.

The evidence of this mindset can be heard through comments like "he made me…" "it wasn't my fault…" "everyone did…to me" "I can't…". This kind of talk is called blame-shifting, and it's derived from a useless view of the world. The victim mindset displays itself through self-righteousness, anxiety, and neediness, among other unnecessary qualities. Worst of all, it directly opposes the truth that we are more than conquerors (Romans 8:37).

I have had my own experiences with falling into a victim mindset. When I first transferred to the University of Georgia, I had constant anxiety. I felt lonely, I wasn't sure what I was doing, and I didn't know how to move forward. I didn't know what to do with all of the thoughts rushing toward me or the unsettled feelings that would seem to overtake me.

My first discipler, Grace Thackston, ministered to me through her faithfulness to our weekly meetings. She kept showing up and graciously teaching me how to release my anxiety to God. I hadn't been able to imagine my life without anxiety, but Grace had hope for me. Her faith made peace a possibility for me. Because she lived in freedom, she kindly set me free. She was empowered to release me from chains I was unaware were binding me. The patience and gentleness she cared for me with were evidence of the Holy Spirit leading her in my process of becoming empowered. Sometimes when I feel anxiety resurfacing, I remember driving down Hog Mountain Road in Athens with her and know that God is stronger than my fears.

Another time in my life, chronic stress and a high-pressure situation led me to re-engage with the anxiety and fear I had worked for years to release. A life-long friend of mine struggled to cope with pain. At the end of a workday I received a call that he was having suicidal thoughts and was being admitted to a psychiatric ward for help. I was grateful that my friend chose to learn in his time at the hospital and continues to build up his resilience. The biggest change I have witnessed in him is his decision to replace self-condemning and judgmental thought patterns with grace for himself and others.

Even as he progressed in mental health, I stayed trapped in fear. The thought of him taking his life would haunt me in the middle of my workday. Any calls I would receive from someone in our circle of friends immediately instilled a sense of panic in me. Focusing on tasks, feeling calm, and getting enough sleep were elusive concepts for weeks. The thoughts I experienced were by no means taken captive and submitted to Christ (2 Corinthians 10:5); they were destructive, uncontrolled, and highly deceptive.

During a Wednesday night ministry service, the speaker mentioned suicide. This triggered my anxiety into high gear. In panic, I sat on the floor in the back of the room and tears streamed down my face silently. A friend sat by me to comfort me and a couple more joined during worship at the end of the message. I hardly felt any relief by the end. My need for help was apparent, so I set up a counseling appointment the next morning. My counselor wasn't available for a few weeks, so I also signed up for an inner healing prayer appointment with a ministry I trusted. I told my mentor the intimate details of my struggling thought life and asked my roommate to hold me accountable to getting out of bed in the morning.

In most places I've sought out inner healing, a similar experience takes place. I sit in a private room with two or three other Christians. They ask for as many specifics as I'm comfortable sharing related to the reason I signed up for inner healing. In this meeting, I told them about how much I love that close friend of mine and how afraid I was that he would die. The rest of the session is spent praying together, asking Jesus to bring up memories or thought patterns that trigger pain, and asking for Him to reveal His love. Oftentimes as we pray, I will be reminded of a Bible verse or have an impression of what God might be saying about the situation based on His character and His Word. This time I felt God impress upon me that He wanted me to let go of my judgment and fears over my friend's life decisions and trade them for a more selfless love and genuine acceptance.

Through inner healing, I recognized the steps I would need to take to regain authority over my mind. I identified lies I was believing about my situation, myself, and God. "My life is destined for chaos and bad things" was a lie. "I am overlooked" was a lie. "God helps others but not me" was a lie.

I discovered hope in God's character that was more dependable than hope in people or situations. I set my mind on the truth that God is trustworthy. He cares for the ones I love. Anytime my friend called and I was unavailable, I challenged myself to let his calls go to voicemail as a statement to myself that I was not solely responsible for his life. Every time I needed to combat the fears keeping me up at night that he might always struggle with suicidal thoughts, I reminded myself that God restores what I fear could be lost.

I refreshed myself with the reality that God dwells within me, so I can be at peace and share peace with my friend when we interact. The pressure was not on me anymore to say the right things or ask the right questions. I was able to accept the invitation to love him well through Christ because Christ already paid for his freedom. His healing wasn't something I needed to work for and earn for him; it was something I could walk with him towards with patient endurance.

Time does not heal; it only provides distance. Passive time leads to repression; active time leads to healing. We have a responsibility to care for ourselves after receiving an emotional wound, just like we would with physical injuries. Meeting with a counselor is one of the ways I actively chose to spend my time, and it has contributed to my emotional healing from that panic-ridden period in many ways.

Counseling was beautifully empowering for six months as I sorted through coping mechanisms, stress tolerance, and the truth of the Word. I uprooted thoughts that were producing bad fruit in my relationships (Matthew 7:17-18). I redesigned the patterns by which I lived my life and was transformed by the renewing of my mind. For example, if I believed that I was going to lose a loved one, then I redirected my thoughts to believe that I am blessed to have loved ones in my life. If I believed I couldn't deter my friend from a harmful lifestyle, then I redirected my thoughts to believe that there was no pressure on me to change him. Rather, my responsibility lies in being accountable for my life and loving others well from confidence in who I am.

Empowerment not only brought me peace but also confidence to be in my friends' "messes" without trying to fix them because I was no longer in a mad rush to make them better. Some healing takes time. God is patient in His power to bring thorough healing. I can be the same as I trust that the Spirit in me is stronger than the forces around them. The accumulating anxiety over my loved ones' decisions dissipated as I lived in confidence that I am secure in God and my life has an influence on those around me.

Our brains have mirror neurons that mimic the neural impulses (emotions) of the person who has our attention. They are what make us yell at the television while watching a quarterback fumble or cry when we sit with a friend through a hard time. This means that as I live in serenity from God, the people looking at me may be able to experience the peace I hold. Think of it like how a small, calm woman can de-escalate the raging anger of her husband with just a glance. I can instill the safety I feel concerning my life and my loved ones into those around me by just being at peace and empathetic.

Paul the Apostle asks us to be gentle and humble, patient and bearing with one another in love (Ephesians 4:2). All of those are in opposition to the human tendency to control or manipulate for desired results. But as we embrace the Spirit inside us, we receive access to loving how He loves. We can be gentle rather than abrasive. We can be humble rather than forceful. We can be patient rather than hurried. We can bear with others in love rather than in conditions and stipulations. Professional counseling provided that for me, and I want to offer that to those around me. I want to live in a way that guides my loved ones toward safe, effective paths to discover what holds them back and how they can move forward.

Living empowered has come and gone in waves. After six months of pursuing emotional well-being, small things in my life started unravelling. Small struggles snowballed into larger trials, and I found myself tangled in anxiety again, twenty pounds underweight, and desperately hopeless. I knew that I was living from the belief that bad things will always happen. The more I conquer, the harder my life will be. The more I press on, the more I will have to press through.

My pastor, my mentor, and my counselor all noticed this twisted revelation I was choosing to live by. I had no idea how to overcome this constant fear of bad things happening because intimidation was pulsing from my recent experiences. Life will not be easy, and even when it improves, it is bound to get worse again. This Ecclesiastes-esque worldview dimmed the light I had been walking in. I felt lost.

My counselor did not deny that life can be hard and will again be hard, but he did not leave me hopeless in that reality. He didn't reject my experiences. Instead, he equipped me with better truth to understand my situation. He strengthened me to see reality as an empowered woman. My counselor called me out for using pessimism as a defense mechanism. I chose to anticipate bad things to protect myself from being caught off guard when they came along. This was self-preservation I had the choice to cling to or let go of. He told me I had every right to live that way, but it comes at a cost. I was cashing in my joy to protect myself when instead I could cash in my self-preservation to receive joy.

Joyful people are empowered people. They are the ones who have chosen to let go of control: control of the people around them, control of what they know, and control of their circumstances. Instead, they live in trust: trust that God is good, trust that they are loved, and trust that they can love freely. I had been trying to control my future and the impact I might suffer by guarding myself with anxiety. My counselor helped me realize that living empowered requires letting go of control and letting life happen. Good and bad will come and go. In my life, I've noticed neither is ever fully absent in a given moment. We live in an imperfect world starving for goodness.

Since I began rejecting my self-preservation mindset, I have felt exposed and insecure. I have also been able to know God more as my Defender. I know He helps me sense His presence when I'm scared or sad. I know He will work all things together for my good when it looks like things are falling apart. I know He lives to intercede for me—that He is consistently working on my behalf. His Word brings me peace when I am experiencing unsettling feelings. His Spirit offers comfort by letting me sense His nearness when I feel alone. I trust Him to come through for me, and He does.

Now, as bad things explode around me, I hurt but I heal. Stress isn't a primary reaction anymore. I am able to be present where I need to be. I make the decision between self-preservation and joy, and I accept the consequences of my choice. Empowerment wasn't free of cost, but the freedom that comes from living empowered is priceless.

Identifying victim mindsets leads people away from self preservation and into the empowerment that God has for them. The last thing someone who is feeling powerless needs is to be accused. Jesus boldly addressed this temptation when He called His followers hypocrites for pointing out the speck in others' eyes while ignoring the plank in their own (Matthew 7). He was and is the only Righteous One. We have to receive freedom as we start asking others to embrace freedom. That way, we are encouraging rather than judgmental or impatient as we walk alongside them into freedom.

As we begin to recognize the victim mindsets in ourselves and others, we should remember the grace that has rescued us into freedom and empowerment. The ways in which we go about encouraging others away from victimization should be Spirit-led and Spirit-filled: marked by love, joy, peace, patience, kindness, goodness, gentleness, faithfulness, and self control (Galatians 5).

Empowered by Truth
Information is power; it's currency. The more you know, the more you can influence a situation. We trust experts in their fields to lead the way because they know more. We trust the advice of older mentors because they've learned through having more experiences. Even socially we gain power over one another by knowing secrets. Truth is the most reliable information. The more truth I have to stand on, the more confident I feel standing.

In college, I would rarely answer questions in a math class. Why? I know very little about math. Science made sense to me, though. I thought it was fascinating. The confidence I had in my understanding of the subject led me to speak up more, which led to a better grade and having more influence in the class. Other students wanted to be in my group for projects because they knew I could handle it. My professors were happy to meet with me because they recognized I cared about my education. My math classes never got to see that side of me. Having truth about God and what He thinks under my belt, I'm more confident and influential. I am more empowered. People are comfortable trusting what I say about God, and leaders are willing to entrust their knowledge of truth with me.

Jesus is truth (John 14). One of the things I love about Him is that He never conveyed that He wants me to be weak and helpless so He can use me or manipulate me. He made me royalty alongside Himself (Revelation 1). In His extravagant love, He gave Himself to me to empower me. He laid down His life so I could step into my destiny. His words and His leadership guide me into influence, confidence, and authority. His truth is my rock.

When hard things take place, words may fall short of comforting or providing relief. Nothing can be said to make what is wrong right again. When anger, confusion, grief, and fear seem to wall me in, sometimes I can't find peace in even the most heart-felt sentiments of a friend. Instead, I meditate on the truth that God is near to the broken-hearted and His nearness is my good (Psalm 34:18; Psalm 73:28).

For me, those truths trump every lie, every fear, and every misunderstanding. I have found in the last three years of my life that the goodness of God is the sole dependable redemption in every situation I have faced. I don't expect everyone to overcome obstacles with God the way that I do. We are all made uniquely and have our own relationships with God that look different from each other. But I do believe there is at least one aspect of God's character that every person can discover which will be an unshakable foundation in their lives.

The Word is the best place to start discovering foundational truth. The process is easy. I like to break down Scripture bit by bit, acknowledging how each piece applies to my life. Ephesians 6 is a commonly known passage of Scripture describing the armor of God. Starting in verse 10, the passage says,"Be strong in the Lord and in His mighty power. Put on the full armor of God, so that you can take your stand against the enemy."

Through this verse I learn I am invited to be strong in the Lord and His power. From the very beginning of learning to gain victory, I am taught that it is not by my own strength but by God's. The pressure is not on me, nor is the expectation. I am fully dependent on the strength of His might. I am given full armor, full protection. I can dismiss the fear of being unequipped or unsafe because I have been covered head to toe against all schemes of the enemy. There is no trick play or surprise attack that can steal my identity as "more than a conqueror" (Romans 8:37).

In verse 12, I learn that I'm not opposing a person or group of people. I can trust that God will hold people accountable to their actions, so I don't have to worry about it. I believe Scripture is clear that God is my Judge and my Avenger. Movies are one of the primary ways I hear God apart from the Bible. Sometimes I'll feel inspired to watch a particular movie (other times I'll just randomly pick one), and God reveals metaphors of how the characters or storylines apply to my life.

There is a scene in one of the Marvel movies, Age of Ultron, when Hawkeye tells the Scarlet Witch she can either stay inside and hide or she could go outside and fight. But if she steps outside, she's an Avenger. The scene in this film is one God regularly reminds me of when I am faced with a spiritual battle. I am not forced to fight my battles. I am not merely a soldier in the army of God sent out to be murdered. God has confidence in the authority that He has given me, so I am invited to fight for the reality He offers to me—that I am a co-heir and co-laborer with Christ.

This is my understanding of the Great Commission and Matthew 10:8: "Heal the sick, raise the dead, cleanse the lepers, drive out demons." It's our choice to follow His leadership and, in doing so, engage in spiritual warfare. To engage is to live in a world more like the Kingdom of God because victory has already been promised. God isn't forcing us to work for Him because He needs tasks done. He has empowered us with the Holy Spirit to see the world changed by making disciples, baptizing them, and teaching them what He has commanded us to teach. We aren't fighting flesh and blood—we are inviting them into the family God ordained.

Continuing with Ephesians 6, Paul lists truth as a part of the armor of God. So I ask myself, "How is truth able to help me?" Truth combats lies that we believe and can disarm the deceiving thoughts we are presented with. I like to find the truth of the Word, either written or spoken, that aligns with the nature of God and meditate on it. I focus on its implications and use it as a default when I feel too weak to move forward. If all goes wrong, and I feel like I'm losing, I go back to the truth and repeat it over myself until I regain strength. Empowerment by truth looks like taking God at His word because His word is life and truth (John 14:6).

Next, Paul describes the breastplate of righteousness. Like I mentioned early on, I had defined righteousness as the desire to do the apparent right thing. We assume if something seems right, it probably is right. But that's not always the case. My friend Kelly uses the story of Mary and Martha from Luke 10 to explain this idea. Martha was doing the apparent right thing, preparing the house and food for Jesus's visit, but it wasn't the "right" thing Jesus wanted from her. Mary was sitting at the feet of Jesus and learning from Him, which her sister condemned her for. But that's what Jesus honored Mary for doing.

I am learning that righteousness is both circumstantial and absolute. It is what God is asking you to do when He is asking you to do it because He is the Creator and Source of the righteous choice. It may or may not be the most obvious, but it will always be the best one. This part of the armor takes me back to my dependence on the Father. When I choose obedience over assumptions, I follow what the Father says and does (John 5:19). I can talk to Truth Himself and live out of that conversation, replacing the enemy's influence and selfish ambition with the Spirit's wisdom. I know that I am living righteously when I am living by what the Author of Righteousness is asking of me. I have no righteousness apart from Him (Philippians 3:9).

In Deuteronomy, especially chapter 2, I see how closely the Israelites were asked to follow the voice of God. They would walk when He said walk and turn when He said turn. They would only fight when He directed them to. Even though they may have appeared stronger or larger in number, they had no chance of victory apart from God. Neither do I. I ask God to lead me in paths of righteousness because I won't find the way on my own. Submission to the will of God is best. This is not because God is a dictator but because He is wiser.

Continuing on, Paul introduces the sandals shod with the readiness of the Gospel of peace in Ephesians 6. To me, Paul is indicating the purpose of the wars we wage. Wars could mean difficulties we fight to overcome, habits we strive to kick, or prayers we persistently pray. The Good News is that peace is our portion. The end goal is perfect peace: no more injustice, no more pain, no more suffering. All of that is found in Jesus, the Prince of Peace.

I don't have to fight to make a name for myself or to give God something out of His reach; I join the battle in front of me because there is a peace that passes understanding available to all. Jesus did not come to condemn the world but to save it (John 3:17). I apply this truth to my life by believing I am not asked to oppose people who strive to live a "good" life apart from God's righteousness; I am empowered to inject peace into their striving and truth into their misconceptions of being a "good" person. Empowerment is embracing the freedom to free others. Empowerment frees us to embrace what Jesus died for. Empowerment fills us with the desire of the Father, which is to bring all to a knowledge of the truth.

Already we have a few verses to lay down an expansive foundation for our faith. I could go on with the rest of the passage, but I would rather you discover for yourself what it means to be personally empowered by the Word. This is an easy passage to dissect for truth. As you look through Scripture, you will find truth all throughout. We know that "man does not live by bread alone but by every Word that comes from the mouth of God" (Matthew 4:4). The Bible is so much more than a book; it is a source of nurturing, a gift from God.

You can discover the ways God is empowering you outside the written Word as well. Do you sense Him speaking as you watch movies? What about when you're sitting in nature or having conversations with friends? He is in every moment. Wait on the Lord, and you'll find strength; look for Him and be empowered by what you find of Him. Empowerment is an adventure we are invited into, not a goal we achieve by striving.

The beauty of empowerment is that once we are free, we can spread freedom like fire. In a meeting with one of my girls, we were talking about her personal history and the ways she has grown. We discussed how her growth has equipped her with the wisdom to help other people grow. Her freedom was not just for the glory of God or for her own sake but to bring others into freedom (which is also conveniently unto the glory of God). How sad would it be if we found victory over something millions struggle with and kept the secret to ourselves?

My siblings, neighbors, and I loved to play outside when we were young. We would play a version of tag in which you would be sent to "jail" if you got tagged. If one person managed to tag the jail before getting caught, all the prisoners would go free. Welcome to the Kingdom where it's exactly the same. Reflect on how you have grown in the many seasons of your life and which areas of life you have found victory over. People are in need and you hold the cure. You are enough, your experience is enough, and even partial knowledge of the truth is enough. In every way we fall short, He will come through.

Free People Free People
When I started noticing how empowered I felt living in the freedom Jesus gave me, I was quick to get prideful. I thought that if I could live in freedom, anyone else could get free. And why wouldn't they get free if it was available to them? And why didn't they listen to me when I tried to help them? I leaned into self-righteousness and judging others, especially others who I thought should know better. The Lord was kind to convict me through reminding me of my past.

I was so blind to the authority that Jesus died for me to use for years, and it was only by the grace of God that I became aware of my inheritance in Christ. Now, as I grow stronger, I can choose to look upon those who are struggling with pity or compassion. I like who I am better when I engage with compassion.

Triggered

People have different triggers when it comes to interpersonal relationships. Once someone told me she loves to serve and that gratitude is important to her. Over the holidays, if her family acts entitled or is too busy to say thank you, she feels crushed. Another time, I was interviewing students at UGA about diversity. One student was particularly passionate about people of different abilities. She shared that when she walks into an inaccessible environment, it breaks her heart because able-bodied people don't realize their lack of understanding is blinding them from aiding someone in need.

We were all uniquely made, which means we will have different emotional triggers and different passions. We can still lend space in our lives to the people who are different from us by meeting together and treating one another with mutual respect, and honor. We need each other. Accepting people for who they are—strengths and weaknesses, faults and victories—is a part of loving well. Our passions and our frustrations are indications of what we were created for. They will expose our weaknesses, but they will also motivate us toward freedom. We can embrace different people's passions with support and weaknesses with grace because they carry keys to freedom that we may never hold without them.

We shouldn't ignore the parts of people we don't like. We should grow in learning to embrace unique qualities in ourselves and others. Awareness of our differences is our gateway to making a difference. Awareness of others' pain is our doorway to bringing healing. Telling someone with a wounded leg that everyone has their hurts or that other people don't have legs at all is insensitive and doesn't actually help. The people you see hurting on the side of the road are the people God has gifted you with to see miracles through.

The priest and the Levite passed by the hurting man on the side of the road before the Samaritan stepped in to graciously help him (Luke 10). How tragic that the supposed "holiest men of Israel," the ones believed to be closest to God, were the ones who ignored the man that Jesus highlighted in that parable. Devoting our lives to God should produce abundance that overflows into the lives around us. Being set apart doesn't mean God desires for us to separate ourselves from others to get closer to Him; we were redeemed from this fallen world so we can love God and one another miraculously. We are empowered to reveal Him to those who are desperate for Him.

Pride disguises itself in self-righteousness and is incredibly dangerous because the self-righteous don't often recognize they're living that way. I fear being covertly prideful and I fight insecurity that I am self-righteous. But I have to remind myself that fear and insecurity are not my portion. They are not gifts from God for me. They are not a part of my identity as a child of God or part of my inheritance in Christ. I have to focus on love and humility because I can't control my reputation, only my character.

If the ones I love call me out for being a hypocrite, I will take a moment to pray and provide space for the Holy Spirit to convict me. To reject the fear of man and insecurity that arises, I welcome the conviction of the Spirit. Oftentimes, I am self-righteous. I have to relearn how to live humbly and change my false view of God that He is fixated on my performance. If I have been following the Spirit, loving genuinely, and still receive criticism, I have to release my need to prove myself to others and change my perception that people's opinions are more important than God's.

What is the point of being here in a broken and beautiful world if not to love? God could have wiped out the world with a flood or with fire. He could say a word, and we would cease to exist. But through Abram, Noah, Moses, John the Baptist, Jesus, Paul, Peter, you, and me, the world is given chance after chance to know the love and life of God. We are witnesses of the Hope of the Nations. We are bearers of peace in the already-won war for this chaotic world. We are evidence of the promise of eternity to this dying world. Don't miss out on that because you don't want to soil your white robes or be late for a service. Love is a stronger force, a stronger Person, than everything else. Please don't miss out on that. Don't hold out on others. They need it as much as you do.

In finishing the parable of the Good Samaritan, Jesus commands, "Go and do likewise." How different, how much stronger and more beautiful would our lives be if we woke up every day to live out that instruction? Imagine a Church like that. Imagine a family who pursued that. Imagine how the lost and broken could truly know love if we embraced that. It is not our responsibility; it is our honor and our privilege as the empowered children of God.

Taking Thoughts Captive

Jessica Longino, a leader I've mentioned before, taught me about discerning between truth and lies at the beginning of my first year on staff in ministry. She taught me that my past perceptions of the world and the events I've experienced contribute to my current view of God.

For example, growing up I didn't have many friendships with girls that lasted more than a year or two. The quick turnover of relationships led me to live like female friendships weren't worth investing in because I believed the lie that they don't last. I had to first redeem my poor perception of women and those experiences of short-term friendships in order to choose a different perspective about friendships. Now my group of girlfriends have been around for years because I don't instinctively check out after a year or two due to past disappointments. When I start to feel distant from them, I reach out and catch up again. I get to experience the joys of long-term friendship, like shared histories and experiences, knowing each others' stories, and pushing each other to live to our full potential.

Taking our thoughts captive and submitting them to God can change our schema. We can dig up our beliefs from our earliest memories onward and align them with truth. This process does not create a distortion of our past or delusion of our experience, but rather, it leads the way we understand our life experiences into alignment with an eternal perspective. We can find God in every moment of our histories and let His truth decide how we perceive the world around us.

When I was twelve years old, my parents gathered my siblings and I in the family room and told us they were getting divorced. I spent the next six years living back and forth between their houses. They lived far enough away from each other that my friends from my mom's city didn't really want to visit while I was at my dad's and vice versa. This resulted in embracing a close friendship with loneliness. I fought hard not to live a double life, but maintaining the same persona as a teenager around different people in different environments was challenging.

A few months into my parents' divorce, I was sitting in my room at my mom's house praying. I felt God impress the truth of Psalm 27:10 in my heart: though my father and mother forsake me, He will receive me. My dad couldn't always be around, and my mom wasn't available all the time either. My friends were mostly incapable of being there for me as well because none of us had licenses. But God was always with me. I started thinking through every moment I felt lonely since the divorce, and knew God was with me in every moment. Without knowing it, I had dug up the lie that I was lonely and aligned it with the truth that God is always with me. With this moment of revelation, I was able to let go of loneliness. Developing my identity didn't feel like a dual process anymore because God was constant as my Father and my closest Friend.

I was talking to one of my girls about how I can now identify the thoughts that come into my mind naturally. In the years I've practiced the discipline of taking thoughts captive, I developed the ability to become aware of each train of thought running through my mind. I feel capable of dealing with them as I wish.

For example, I felt anxiety as I was falling asleep one night. I didn't have a specific fear that I was aware of, but I felt paranoid just about being home alone. Within seconds of monitoring my train of thoughts, I was able to identify the thought that something might go wrong while I was asleep. Just as quickly, I decided that's not highly realistic or necessary. I live in a safe neighborhood, no crimes have happened lately, I have a security system, and a very large, scary-looking dog. Within minutes, I was sleeping peacefully.

Some anxious thoughts may not be as easy to dismiss. I remember being on a plane a few years ago and the turbulence was so intense that it felt like we were dropping hundreds of feet at a time. The rocky ride lasted significantly longer than I was comfortable with. The panicked energy from the people around me only increased the stress I was feeling. Men and women much older than me were closing their eyes and stifling gasps as we dropped and rose.

Because I'm not a pilot, I couldn't do anything to help. I realized my panic wasn't helping the situation or my well-being. I

For My Girls

chose to be at peace with the fact that I would either be physically okay or not at the end of the day, but the final outcome was out of my control. So I unclenched my jaw, released the tension from my shoulders, and took a deep breath. I focused my mind on Jesus—that loving Man who died so I could live with Him forever. It didn't make the turbulence fun, but it quieted my soul. Having survived (praise God), I'm glad I didn't waste all my time up there turning my hair gray with worry.

Lies are deceptive and overlooking them can feel natural. But deception only has power until you've identified it. Once you understand the illusion, you stop falling for the magician's tricks. When I can't discern the lie that's producing things like anxiety, fear, anger, and so on, that's when I phone a friend. My girlfriends, discipler, and parents are quick to help with their outside perspectives. Their questions and listening ears hold incredible power. Some helpful questions for times like these have been:

> When did you start feeling this way?
>
> What caused you to feel this way?
>
> What is one thought going through your mind right now?
>
> Do you think it's related to [any event that they knew was challenging for me]?
>
> What do you need?
>
> What do you think God is saying?
>
> What do you remember the Bible says about [fear, anger, sadness, etc.]?

Eventually the lie comes out. I started feeling insignificant because someone offended me, but God says I'm significant. I believed my future was uncertain, but God has made my path secure. I fear moving away and making new friends, but God made me unique and created people to connect with one another. Maybe my fear was related to a hard meeting I had. Maybe I

140

need the peace of God but I'm believing the lie that I don't have access to peace. Maybe God is saying that I am living out of insecurity when He has already given me purity, beauty, and confidence. Maybe resting in the Bible's truth that I can cast my cares on Jesus can change the entire situation. The helpful questions my close friends and family have asked me are just a few open doors to valuable, freeing conversations.

Despite the difficulty of battling anxious thoughts, I have to remind myself that anxiety does not have more power over me than I have in the Holy Spirit. Whether on this side of death or the other, I will overcome. I can wait on the Lord, and He will renew my strength (Isaiah 40:31). When my mind races with anxiety, I can trust God will still be with me when it passes. When my mind goes into a blank fog of anxiety, I can trust God will whisper comfort to me until I am clear-headed again. Any win is a win when it comes to overcoming habitual thought patterns. One day I'll string together enough victories that I won't even feel the sting of all the struggle it took to get there. Your mind is yours, and it is God's. You may always have the temptation to entertain ungodly thoughts, whatever those are for you, but you will not always feel weak facing them.

In a discipleship meeting with one of my girls, I was sharing the revelation I received earlier that morning during a staff quiet time. If the enemy can't convince you of a lie, he'll convince you the truth doesn't matter. The most deceptive lies couldn't persuade me that God wasn't near me in my pain, so the next best thing was for the enemy to convince me that His nearness doesn't matter. But it does. During that quiet time, I completed a self-awareness exercise. I let my imagination run wild then considered why I imagined the things I had. Typically the events I imagine in some ways reflect fears, hopes, expectations, and perceptions I am holding on to. This particular morning I had imagined myself laying defeated in pain and God just standing by passively watching. This vain imagination conveyed that God didn't care that I was hurting, and His supposed indifference made me want to disconnect even further from Him.

Why would I run to God if I believe He doesn't do anything when I'm feeling broken? My perspective of God acting disengaged with my suffering does not align with what I've read in Scripture, so instead I began imagining God holding me in a tight hug as I cried. This imagination is more in line with His real character. The thought of His gentle embrace made me want to draw nearer to Him. I believed I could find peace in Him. He is my comforter. I don't want to dwell on thoughts or imaginations that exalt themselves against the knowledge of God (2 Corinthians 10:5). I want to redirect my mind toward the truth. Feelings are not truth; they are indicators of your perception. Pay attention to what your feelings are telling you. Is something good? Is something off? What are you believing about it? What does God have to say about it? What does the Bible have to say about it? Our feelings are quick to reveal instinctual responses to people and situations, and equally as quick to deceive us. They are tools, not foremen, in the construction of our worldviews.

Empowered by Grace

The girls I have discipled are incredible, highly capable young women. A few of them are exceptionally service-minded and live insanely full lives. From early in the morning until very late in the night, they give themselves to working hard and caring for people well. As impressive as they are, they are not impervious to the temptation to strive. They have to be intentional not to let their work turn into a way validate their worth, form their identities, or earn favor before God. This leads to many amazing conversations about grace.

Grace is deeply intertwined with empowerment. It is the generous gift of God's favor that redeems us into salvation and transforms us into holiness. I've noticed that when I am living in sin or tripping repeatedly on the same stumbling block, I don't feel like I'm living up to my highest potential. In these moments, every connection I pursue with God is either conviction or correction that I'm wrestling Him over. I realize how futile it is to argue with God over sin. But it works for my relationship with God to discuss with painful honesty how I feel about the sin I'm struggling with.

God and I have long conversations about how the sin is not working in my favor or how it is in opposition to His character. Blindly accepting God at His word is a good thing. If He doesn't answer me when I complain about how I want to watch a trashy television show that I keep getting convicted over and over about, it will still be wrong for me to keep watching that show. But in His kindness toward me, He usually explains what in the show He doesn't want me seeing and how it's negatively affecting my life.

For example, I once watched a documentary on Ted Bundy. I knew that I was sensitive to violence and choosing a different show would have prevented needless fear, but I chose to ignore that wisdom and watch anyway. The creativity of the violence Ted Bundy incurred on all those people produced fear in me that people like that exist. Even the charm through which he persuaded people disturbed me. When I felt unsettled halfway through the film and the remainder of the day, I felt God's correction and His compassion for me.

The Holy Spirit brought to mind His hatred toward evil. I realized my sensitivity was conviction for entertaining myself with something God hates. He was with me the whole time I was engaging in something that grieved Him. He loved every single one of those victims, and I was watching a retelling of it just to have something to do. I felt Him remind me that I don't have to do things that make me uncomfortable to fit in or to be "in the know." I like that about my relationship with God. Even my wrongdoings, after I repent, bring me closer to Him. I get to know more about Him through hearing why He hates what He does. He makes all things new. His redemption is far more powerful than our failures.

Grace is the training ground on which we learn to conquer sin. Grace is the permission to live in the power of God and the victory of the Resurrection. Grace sees you coloring on the wall with a marker as a child and says, "You can't do that, baby, but I'll fix it with you." Then you buy a can of paint together and bond over correcting the issue. God is love, and love covers a multitude of sins (1 Peter 4:8). For us, sin is a big deal. It's messy, it's scary, it harms us, it breaks God's heart, and it makes Him angry. But God is not intimidated by sin.

I think of the scene in the beginning of Lion King when Simba goes to the elephant graveyard with Nala, despite his father's instructions. Mufasa, Simba's father, has to rescue the two of them from the hyenas. As the hyenas are about to attack, Mufasa roars in a terrifying display of power and brings his children from outside of their boundaries into the safety of his kingdom. The danger is real. The rage in the father's heart is undeniably real. But there is no question of who has more power. Grace gave us a relationship with the Father similar to Mufasa and the cubs. His favor toward us as His children empowers us to live outside of the bondage of sin and in the protection of the loving Father (Titus 2:11-12).

The sins in our lives hold us back and they directly defy God. It is necessary to recognize that sin hurts us, but it is selfish to only acknowledge sin as something that affects us—sin breaks the heart of God. God hates sin. We must remember that, in His love, God also hates. Proverbs 6:16-19 shares a list seven things the Lord hates: "haughty eyes, a lying tongue, and hands that shed innocent blood, a heart that devises wicked plans, feet that make haste to run to evil, a false witness, and one who sows discord."

Throughout Scripture, you'll discover that God detests evil. He instructs us to hate the evil He hates (Proverbs 8:13). Don't let this revelation of God swallow up the rest of your knowledge of God. He is not either a Father who loves and delights or a Father who hates and is angry. He is a multifaceted, emotional, living Father. Even His anger and His hatred are good because He is the origin of goodness.

I love hanging out with girlfriends and chatting. But I hate sitting around complaining about our bodies. You'd be surprised how often conversations like that come up. At the gym, in the bathroom, by the pool—all easy places to fall into self-hatred and insecurity. If you want to connect with me, it's not going to be over how ugly we feel. It's not because I don't want to connect, it's because I hate when we tear ourselves down.

My friends don't talk that way around me much. When someone does, I am quick to encourage my friend to run back to God's standard of self-respect and love. I don't turn into a different person or abandon my friends because of their decisions to engage in something I don't enjoy; they'll just get to know more about who I am by the strong feelings I have toward how we talk about ourselves. They know that connecting with me and talking badly about themselves are mutually exclusive. Similarly, God hates some things and refuses to allow us to bring them into our relationships with Him. It's not a mystery; it's all laid out in Scripture. A loving person cannot advocate for evil. It makes sense that the most loving Being hates evil.

Grace brings us into relationship with God, which, in effect, takes us out of relationship with sin. This doesn't mean Christians can't sin but that people who actively abide in God will not actively abide in sin. God is the One who empowers us; grace is the river that carries us into more power. We have access to a life without the lack that habitual sin creates in us. Sin leads to death (James 1:15), and partnering with or participating in it steals, kills, and destroys. But Jesus gave us more (John 10:10). He gave us abundant life in Him. We don't need to let sin direct our lives, whether it's a one-time mistake or a life-long addiction. We are empowered to walk in freedom.

I was in a discipleship meeting, listening to one of my girls talk about when Peter walked on water, when it dawned on me that Peter didn't walk on water for a very long time. I realized that Peter only walked until the wind blew, then he began to sink. Immediately, Jesus reached out, caught him, and helped him climb into the boat. We sometimes confuse miracles with success. Grace is our security that even if we don't make it to land walking on water, we can try to respond to Jesus when He calls and trust Him to rescue us if we start to sink. Peter was empowered by what he was witnessing Jesus do and stepped out in faith. He failed when he saw the wind, even though he was already walking on water. He got his miracle and lost it. But I hear this story and see victory because Peter tried. Empowerment doesn't always mean succeeding. Sometimes it means sinking and seeing that God will put you right back in a secure place. You're safe to take risks. Even if fear comes and you momentarily look away from Jesus, He will rescue you. That is the beauty of grace. Take a chance on Him.

I have met many Christians concerned that believers will be drawn astray by doctrines of "too much grace." I think those who abuse grace misunderstand grace. More specifically, I think those who are abusing grace are actually not receiving the grace they have been offered. They embrace a myth that grace is a never-ending pardon for unrighteous behavior rather than a gift of forgiveness that reunites us with our Holy God. They are not actually living in grace but in the lie that God cares more about us having a clean slate than being in a relationship with Him. The "grace" they are abusing is a deception tactic from the enemy to keep us blind to our loving Father. Throughout Scripture, I see God as an abundantly gracious God rather than a cautiously gracious God. He, the God of all grace, sits on a throne of grace (1 Peter 5:10; Hebrews 4:16). He longs to be gracious and has freely justified us by grace (Isaiah 30:18; Romans 3:23-24). Romans 5 and 6 help us understand the relationship between sin and grace more clearly. Paul says:

> "...Where sin increased, grace increaseded all the more, so that, as sin reigned in death, so also grace might reign through righteousness to bring eternal life through Jesus Christ our Lord. What shall we say then? Shall we go on sinning so that grace may increase? By no means!"

In simplified terms, we were slaves to our sin before coming alive in Christ, and now we are under the reign of grace. We were made righteous and are led on paths of righteousness. Grace unlocks a door to righteousness. You don't recklessly sin and cover it up with grace. You recklessly sin and are revived into repentance and righteousness by grace.

Paul continues in the chapter saying, "for sin shall no longer be your master, because you are not under the law, but under grace." Grace is an entirely new justice system in which we are freely favored because we are made perfect and being made holy (Hebrews 10:14).

My own meditations on grace have brought me to this understanding: grace is about purpose and belonging, not reward and pardon. The parable of the laborers in the vineyard that Matthew 20 describes is where I uncovered this understanding of grace. The master of the vineyard goes out multiple times a day hiring laborers and pays them all the same amount, regardless of the time they spent working for him. The earliest laborers are understandably irritated at the seemingly unfair equality that has been distributed, but the master of the house reminds them he was fair. He gave them exactly what they had agreed upon.

Then he asks them, "Are you envious that I am generous?" Another translation says, "Are you jealous that I am kind?" The master of the vineyard, representing the Father, hired people who were idle in the streets. He gave them something to do just like God gives us purpose. He gave them someone to work for just like God gives us belonging. He doesn't give work for the sake of work just like He doesn't give payment for the sake of debts owed. He didn't give us grace as a reward in spite of our sin or as an excuse to sin. He gives us grace because grace leads us into purpose and belonging.

If you think about your salvation, you weren't just redeemed from slavery to death and sin. You were transformed into a new life and adopted into royalty. You now have a more generous inheritance, a more influential role, and a more loving family. The saving grace Jesus extended to all of us was never solely to give us a clean conscience, but to live out our identities as His joy (Hebrews 12:2). We were once covered in sin, the very thing God hates. By grace, we are now the ones who bring delight to His heart (Psalm 16:3).

As someone who has been a believer longer than I can remember, I feel the temptation to resent God for being so gracious toward others or resent others for abusing grace. But I hear God say to me, "Are you jealous that I am generous?"

I would like to aim my life in the same direction as Paul: only to finish the race and complete the task the Lord Jesus has given me—the task of testifying to the good news of God's grace (Acts 20:24). Testifying to God's grace should look good, feel good, and be good because it is good. Accountability in righteousness is necessary, but grace shouldn't have to come with a list of stipulations. It can be explained for exactly what it is, and that will suffice. At the very center of the message of grace, we will find Jesus Christ descending from heaven, laying in a manger, living in power, dying on a cross, rising from the dead, ascending to the Father, and giving us His Spirit—all on His own accord. "It is by grace you have been saved, through faith—and this is not from yourselves, it is the gift of God—not by works, so no man can boast" (Ephesians 2:8-9)." He provides more than enough grace for us all.

Empowered in Relationships

Since God established unity, love, and marriage, the enemy strongly fights to disrupt these things. Healthy, holy relationships are a reflection of our relationships with God, and what a beautiful expression of the heart of God that is for the world to see.

Feeling weak, powerless, unheard, unseen, or vulnerable in relationships is not our portion as children of God. He has good things for us. I learned in one of my college courses that whoever cares least has the most power in a relationship because they can leave whenever they want to. I want to see a shift in our understanding of power in relationships so that instead of the least invested person having the most power, it's the person most confident in the love of God. Confidence in God's love produces contentment and an endless resource of powerful love for others.

I was driving in my car one night, just talking with God. He was prodding at these reservoirs of love in me that I was protecting to only share with specific people. I had a pool of love inside me saved for a husband and children. I had a pool of love for a relative I had just lost. I had pools of love for each of my girls. These mental pools contained ideas for how to care for them, what boundaries I established with them, and how often I felt I could interact with them.

A song came on in the car with the lyrics, "Your love will not run empty. Your love's a well that will never run dry." I realized that I needed to surrender the love I was saving up for people and simply receive God's love—for me and for them. God's love is better than mine. It has no selfish ambition and no need for validation. God's love is endless and covers a multitude of sins, while mine is limited and only as gracious as I feel on any given day.

The reserves of love I had been protecting can actually overflow as I abide in Love. Letting Him fill me every day protects me from the fear of not having enough. My relationships, past, present, and future, are preserved by God's enduring love.

I think it's important to recognize when we try to love people out of our own strength. In my experience, it leads to bitterness or neediness. Instead of loving freely, we save up our love as a rare resource. When someone can't or doesn't receive it, we are heartbroken. But when our souls are vessels for the ever-abundant eternal love of God, the resource is not rare anymore—just priceless.

We are empowered to love generously. We can care deeply and not be afraid of what might hurt someday. God is our first Love and more than enough. The stakes aren't high anymore when we live in light of that truth. We are loved. We are cared for. We are pursued by Love.

I tell my girls to approach relationships with what they want in mind and to keep that as the focus. Asking "Do I still want this relationship?" is a better route to take in your thought life than "Does he still want me?" The point of dating is to discover if you want to keep dating, and, eventually, if you want to keep doing life together long-term. Insecurity, pressure, fighting for attention, or settling for less isn't what God has for us in our relationships. You can identify these issues in many different ways: passive aggressive comments, jealousy, constant arguing, loss of self, socially withdrawing, feeling like you don't deserve better, or wishing he would break up with you because you don't feel like you can. Those things may happen, but they should not be a normal part of your relationship. We should be at peace in relationships that are blessed by God and explore relationships from the security of His faithfulness.

The best relationship advice I can offer is to love wildly, inevitably get hurt, then love again. Sow seeds of love instead of storing them up and letting them be stolen or rot. Jesus said that unless a kernel of wheat falls to the ground and dies, it remains only a single seed, but if it dies, it produces many seeds (John 12). It's scary to let something go and see if it grows. But we won't know unless we try. There's not as much to lose as we think most of the time. If a relationship doesn't turn out like you had hoped, everything will be okay. For all of eternity you'll get to live in the perfect love of your Creator.

In this life, your heart may break when relationships change or fall apart. Letting the love of God flow through you is never a waste. Have boundaries and be wise, but don't hold back in fear. We are secure in the love of God. We don't have to hoard love like it's a scarce resource; God's love is a well that will never run dry. We are provided for and protected.

Boundaries

Boundaries are expectations that distinguish the acceptable from the unacceptable within a given relationship. I explain what boundaries are to my girls the following way: Imagine you are a home. You have your front yard and almost anyone is welcome there if you see them passing by—anyone except stalkers, home invaders, murderers, or registered offenders, of course. Then you have your living room. You can invite anyone you want inside—friends, family, acquaintances, coworkers, and one-time visitors. They get to see things you like, your style, your personality—but not much else. You have a guest room. Your close friends and family can stay there and make themselves at home. They can help themselves to your kitchen and maybe bring a gift in return for your hospitality. They receive from you and you from them. They'll know more about you than newly-acquainted dinner guests. And finally, there's your bedroom. The people closest to you can enter in with an invitation, but no one else. They get to see what no one else sees: the most private, intimate, sacred as-

pects of your soul. If I'm at a ministry event, I can invite the
people there to the metaphorical barbecue in my front yard, but
that doesn't give them access to my metaphorical guest room. I'll
have small talk conversations with them, offer them a prayer or
word of encouragement, or may even give them my phone number to meet up with later if I felt a strong connection to them. But
I don't need to open up about my greatest insecurities with them
or give them all my time, attention and energy for the week.

If I'm with my sister, I feel free to invite her into all the
rooms of my metaphorical house, including my personal, private
sanctuary. She can ask me what's stressing me out, and I can feel
safe to share. She can see me when I'm angry and I can be honest about my greatest struggles. She is someone I can share my
deepest dreams with and wait with me for them to come true.

In the same way that I expect others to respect my boundaries, I want to respect theirs. I don't attend parties or enter into
private conversations without an invitation. I don't ask deep
questions on a first date because I don't belong in a man's
metaphorical (or literal) bedroom when I first meet him. I don't
play with my disciple's hair in our first discipleship meeting (as
if we were in her living room) because she's just met me. Connecting over vulnerability is inevitable, so we need to be careful
with whom we are vulnerable. Self disclosure inspires responsibility from the listener because they now know something that
most people don't.

Intimacy develops through vulnerability. The trouble is when
the depth of the relationship is greater than the length of it. Take
the time to establish your boundaries; love is patient. Think
about the rooms in your house and who you're letting in each
place.

We often see in relationships, especially between parents, a
fun person and a harsh person. Good cop/bad cop ploys become
the boxes we identify ourselves in, whether we like it or not, due
to personality differences. At least one person usually ends up
unhappy. Relationships are a training ground, no matter how
many years we have been in one. We should be learning in all
our relationships, especially romantic ones, to stretch, grow, and
seek to improve rather than relying on our partner's strengths to
balance out our weaknesses.

I offer intentionality in most of my friendships, so my
friends who aren't very intentional can learn that from me. I

show up when I say I'm going to, I make plans when I haven't seen a friend in a while, and I give my full attention to the person I've given my time to. Those are some of the ways I know how to love people well, and hopefully the people I love can learn to love others that way because they know me. I'm not great at comforting people, but my friend, Tori, is amazing at it. So instead of relying on her to be the comforting presence in our friendship, I try to observe how she comforts and emulate those actions in my own relationships. Relationships should make us better, more well-rounded people—not codependent.

There's a lot of personal responsibility involved in building strong relationships. The best thing that we can do is let go of expectations and disappointments and simply love people. We can always call one another higher and remind them of who they are. But we should be ready to offer grace when they make mistakes. For friendships that are healthy, hold on. Hurt has a way of twisting our perceptions and convincing us some people aren't worth it. Every person is worth loving, but not every relationship is worth continuing. We just need to be aware of when relationships have become not only messy but dangerous.

I was sleeping in my room one night when I woke up to a sensation on my cheek. I ignored it and closed my eyes again. Seconds later, I felt the sensation again on my arm. Jumping out of bed, I clicked on my lamp and saw a cockroach disappear into my sea of blankets. Needless to say, I slept in the living room that night.

Don't let people be your cockroaches. Don't be so disgusted by something about them that you avoid them. Maybe you had an unpleasant interaction with someone, and now it's awkward or frustrating to be around them. That's an indication it's time to ask for what God thinks about the person. I promise He has good thoughts for them, even if you come up empty. Even if you recognize the need to create new or stronger boundaries with the person, you can still bless them as you step back. God gives us wisdom through feelings, impressions, advice from trusted friends, or the Bible about when we need to create space between ourselves and unsafe people.

Another time, I was about to go to bed when I saw a scorpion scurry behind my headboard. I didn't sleep until it was dead. If there's a truly harmful relationship in your life, you should end that relationship and seek healing from any damage that was done. Again, relationships should make us better people, not codependent. If you need to end a relationship, you can do that. Some people can be wolves in sheep's clothing or some may be plain, old wolves.

A harmful relationship doesn't necessarily imply the other person involved is evil; it just means their interactions with you produce fear, abuse, or patterns of unhealthy behavior. When navigating an unhealthy relationship, the wisest course of action to take is to minimize or discontinue connection with the person. Unhealthy behaviors include isolation from other friends and family, coercion and threats, monetary manipulation and control, intimidation and fits of rage, and humiliation and lying, just to name a few.

Conversations with older, emotionally stable, trusted mentors can help you differentiate between ending a harmful relationship versus unnecessarily cutting out "toxic" people from your life—as is the trend with the rise of certain emotional health fads. Labeling others as "toxic" is probably not the best way we can live out blessing our enemies and forgiving those who have wronged us. We don't want to get in the habit of distancing ourselves from sinners—that makes us hypocrites. We want to get in the habit of using wisdom in all of our relationships. We can create strong boundaries in harmful relationships without mercilessly judging an individual.

Once, I had a male acquaintance who was looking for friendship, so we would interact every week or so with my unspoken "friendship with a guy" boundaries. For me, that means no late-night hang outs, no getting emotionally deep, and minimal-to-no physical contact. I don't have to communicate upfront, I can just not do those things. If I feel pressured to cross those boundaries, I'm able to say I don't want to. This particular man did not honor those boundaries, so I stopped him when he began asking questions that were too personal or trying to invade my personal space.

When his emotions began fluctuating dramatically as we would interact between pleasantry to pushiness, I created more distance between interactions. When his texting became obsessive, I told him he needed to respect my space. When he showed up at my job unannounced, hiding between security cameras, and pestering me with inappropriate questions, I told him he needed to leave. When he didn't, I called a friend to sit with me until my shift was over. I communicated to him that I wasn't comfortable interacting with him because he wasn't listening to me or respecting my boundaries. I wished him well, but I ended our friendship and didn't respond to his texts anymore.

I don't want to be fake. I really do hope he has a great life. If we ran into each other on the street, I would genuinely smile and wave. But I can't allow people to be close to me who won't respect my boundaries that are an extension of my identity in Christ. My example with that acquaintance is mild compared to what many girls I know have been through. So while I gave him multiple chances to change his behavior, you don't have to extend the same to a person who makes you feel uncomfortable. Your safety is valuable, and people don't have a right to impose on it. Trust is a gift we must give away of our own volition, but once it has been broken, it needs to be earned back. That's okay. Loving people and giving grace—even turning the other cheek—must be used with the gifts of wisdom and discernment.

Is it wise to stay in the relationship being walked over? Is it leading the person toward Jesus, or is it hurting you and potentially leading you towards severe trauma? Is the person just immature and growing, or is there a spirit of malice influencing his or her behavior? Ask God. Ask your close friends and trusted mentors. There is wisdom in a multitude of counselors (Proverbs 11:14). Remember, God's intentions and plans for you are not to harm you. If you think you are in harm's way, it's time to seek wise counsel. Don't gossip; honor well and learn how to use wisdom.

Finding a harmful relationship in your life should be a rare occasion. If it is a common occurrence, that's a good time to start reflecting on yourself. Are there patterns of interacting that you can alter to avoid contributing to unhealthy behaviors in relationships? Is there something lacking inside of you that you are filling with needing to feel needed or having relational drama to distract yourself with? Is it something else? God, a mentor, a close friend can help you recognize relational trends like that. You need outside perspectives. Social scientists have discovered diagnosticity bias, memory bias, selective attention, and sentiment override all blind us to the things we don't want to see in a person. People make mistakes, and although we have grace, we are not bound to relationships that repeatedly tear us down.

Paul encouraged us to live at peace with everyone as far as it depends on us if at all possible (Romans 12:18). Let that be the aspiration and harmful relationships be the rare exception. Jesus gave us excellent instruction on how to handle relationships that are not going well. Talk it out with the person. If the behavior doesn't change, bring a mediator or wise friend into the conversation. If it continues to persist, you can stop your relationship with that person (Matthew 18). Communicating boundaries and holding people accountable doesn't have to be harsh or awkward. Hopefully as you grow in your ability to communicate, it won't be anymore.

My close girlfriends are women who are growing both as individuals and in their relationships with God. They give me permission to call them out when they're not meeting my expectations for our friendship and I give them permission to do the same for me. We are vulnerable with each other and support each other the best way we can. I don't share their secrets and they don't share mine. Our relationships have strengthened and deepened over time, though not all at once on the first day of meeting. The boundaries I've set with my girlfriends are pretty wide. Beyond those boundaries are things like using me or taking advantage of my generosity. I don't have many specific boundaries beyond those with my closest friends because our values are so compatible that we rarely conflict, and we are intentional to communicate with one another if something is wrong. I've given them a lot of freedom in our relationships because I trust them.

I have different boundaries with the girls I disciple. They can tell me anything, and it's confidential—unless they want to harm themselves or another person. They can call or text me any time day or night, but they know my phone is often on "do not disturb," and I won't check it when I'm with someone else or late at night unless it's an emergency. They have given me permission to hold them accountable to their goals, but they don't have the same position in my life. The reciprocity is different with them than with my close friends—not because I love them any less, but because our relationships are of a different nature since I am a mentor-figure in their lives.

I am learning to be more realistic in my expectations and better about communicating when they aren't met. If a friend shares something with others that was very personal to me, I need to tell her privately, in a gentle way, that I do not condone a lack of confidentiality in my relationships. If a friend repeatedly breaks my confidentiality, I will be more cautious with what I share with her. My idealistic expectation is that she won't share my secrets anymore, but reality is that she probably will. So I can establish a boundary by not sharing what I don't want to be public knowledge with friends who prove to be untrustworthy in this area.

I finally recognized after college that most of my relationships were failing because I was inconsistent with my boundaries. I was attracting people who would abuse my kindness because I didn't say no. The problem wasn't that everyone was mean to me—that's a victim mindset. The problem was that I said I had respect for myself, but my choices didn't reflect that. I encouraged people to meet their potential, but I let it slide when they fell short.

I didn't understand that I could tell someone they were wrong and still be loving. But the Holy Spirit, my greatest Friend, demonstrates the perfect example of how to do this. He convicts, but He doesn't condemn. He loves, but He does not tolerate being blasphemed. He is perfectly wise in the way that He loves me and gracious in the ways He calls me to live better. I want to live my life in a way that reflects my identity as a child of God, so I need my behavior to be consistent with my words.

If you look around and realize everyone in your life is imperfect, congratulations. You've discovered the brokenness of the world. Most of them don't need us to write them off but to love them well in our own brokenness. Tell them how to build their own metaphorical houses and manage their own homes. The only one who gets to dwell with you in your house 24/7 is the Holy Spirit. Your responsibility to yourself is to determine, with prayer and wise counsel, which relationships are healthy and which relationships need boundary re-establishments.

Things don't always go as planned. We learn that early on in love. A glory of our salvation is that even when things don't go as planned, God satisfies us. When I lose or end a relationship, I like to ask myself what blessings I received from that relationship and discover how God fills that need for me. He is intimate, passionate, caring, gentle, kind, and supportive. He loves to hear about my day and tell me about the dreams of His heart. As I move through break ups, I don't have to buy into thoughts of loneliness or unworthiness. I know I am loved. Each broken heart takes me deeper into the love of God and closer to a relationship that I can thrive in. I am free to release possession of the ones I love and the things I want. God will give and take any relationship He sees fit; I choose to believe He is good.

Singleness

One of my girls is absolutely beautiful with a stellar personality. She is so easy to love, but she struggled with feeling discontent in her singleness. We talked and prayed about it in a few of our meetings. I was reading through Ezekiel during a staff quiet time one morning when I happened upon chapter 16 and knew God was nudging me to share it with her.

The story here is of the city of Jerusalem. God discovers "her" as a child and raises her in love and provision. He baths her, clothes her, adorns her, and crowns her. She is made famously beautiful because the Lord wanted to make her that way. But she ends up wasting her beauty on men by becoming a prostitute. The rest of the chapter gets pretty dark. Through this story, God showed me that He makes us beautiful because He loves us— not so we can give it away to men or to use it to determine our worth and value. He blesses us with beauty because He thinks we are worthy and lovable. Romantic relationships and marriage are beautiful things, but they are ultimately not what our beauty is intended for. People are beautiful. Creation is beautiful. A blessing of being human is getting to enjoy the beauty that God has woven into the fabric of the universe and all of its inhabitants. But, more than existing for the enjoyment of our beholders, our beauty was given to us to reflect the glory of God; relationships cannot add or detract from that.

I've met many students who are ashamed that they want to get married, and that's sad. Marriage is beautiful. If that's a dream you have, you don't need to be ashamed to admit it. Talk to God about your desires; He cares about the most intimate longings of your heart. I've met just as many students who idolize the idea of marriage. It's not worth it. Idolatry will suck the joy out of your life. It leads to comparison, bitterness, not trusting God, getting hurt in dating relationships, and disconnection from God as you exalt marriage above knowing Him. God is going to take care of you and love you extravagantly. Seek Him first, and everything else will be added to you. You won't be in want (Psalm 23). Trust Him to give when you're ready to receive. Dream with Him. Live with Him.

Loved

On Spring Break 2017, I found myself in an overcrowded small room in Redding, California, bawling like a baby. For the first time, someone had explained to me that sex is a good thing. Or maybe this was just the first time I actually believed it. Life started to make more sense as she taught me that women aren't supposed to people-please and perform for attention. We don't have to compete for intimacy or suppress our desire for connection. We don't have to wait for a husband to establish our worth or a man to give value to our beauty. And, most importantly, we don't have to be afraid.

I had carried a lot of confusion about sex through my adolescence, but it wasn't anyone's fault. I had concocted my own ideas about sex and love from subliminal (and not-so-subliminal) messages in media and social interactions. Those crappy ideas were things like:

Sex is bad.

Sex proves love is real.

Women have to look and act a certain way to be sexy.

Boundaries won't be respected by men.

I left that tiny room with a new courage for my love life. I left with a new passion to redeem the way shame-burdened, fearful, indoctrinated Christian women see themselves. I knew that if God could provide someone to help me see more clearly, God could use me to help others receive the same revelation.

Elephant-Sized

One of my favorite quotes is from Chimamanda Ngozi Adichie, author of We Should All Be Feminists. I've only skimmed her work in a bookstore, but her words play through my mind often.

> "We teach girls to shrink themselves, to make themselves smaller. We say to girls, you can have ambition, but not too much. You should aim to be successful, but not too successful. Otherwise, you would threaten the man...Because I am female, I am expected to aspire to marriage. I am expected to make my life choices always keeping in mind that marriage is the most important. Now marriage can be a source of joy and love and mutual support, but why do we teach girls to aspire to marriage and we don't teach boys the same?"

This passage obviously addresses double standards in society, but I've found many helpful nuggets of truth in it that relate to other social issues. Many girls have been taught to shrink themselves. To be quieter, thinner, gentler. I frequently meet college girls who have struggled with feeling like they are "too much," and I've heard women of all ages complain about their weight my entire life. The dialogue between America and her inhabitants is often that women should be pretty and compliant. Earlier eras' cultural traditions placed greater value on women who suppressed themselves and suffered to perpetuate a facade of perfection over women who could not or chose not to comply. Thankfully, the conversation around a woman's worth has been brought into the light in my lifetime, and I am hopeful to see more change as we move forward.

Let's communicate that women are strong. We are resilient, influential, nurturing, selfless, beautiful, and intelligent. When women embrace their God-given qualities of femininity, the lies of body-perception distortion begin to fade. Loud or quiet, we are valuable. Skinny or curvy, we are beautiful. We no longer need to strive for an unattainable and fickle standard of perfection, but we can live in freedom to pursue health by our own standards. We can work with what works for us.

Men are often overlooked in, but never exempt from, the struggle against restrictive stereotypes. In different ways, they have sustained as many blows from societal expectations as women have. Stereotypes bind them as various interactions reinforce the negative beliefs they have toward themselves. Because we expect men not to emote, we steal their security to express struggles with self-esteem. We silence their self-hatred and push them further into cells that harden them to be more "masculine." What should be communicated is that men are strong. They are emotional, powerful, inspirational, handsome, and capable. When men embrace their masculine qualities, the bondage of shame is broken, and they can celebrate their God-given uniqueness.

One of my favorite animals is the elephant because of their quiet strength and playful nature. On the way home from work one day, my mom texted me a graphic she found of an elephant and the words "be like an elephant: remember what matters, look out for your herd, and don't be afraid to take up space." She didn't know that morning I had co-lead a meeting and, though it went well, I wanted to quit because I felt like my co-leader could do better alone.

Co-leading that meeting the next week with fresh confidence made it one of my favorite meetings of the semester. Some days I'm afraid to take up space. But I think God's desire for me is that I don't shrink down so others can feel big. He created enough space for all of us to be who He has purposed us to be. Nothing will take away our identities that God has established. It doesn't always matter what we do, but who we are will always matter. We are children of God. We become giants in the faith as we grow in our identities rather than in our accomplishments.

Healthy and Sexy

For as long as I can remember, I have been fighting a lifelong battle with my physical health. My sweet tooth came in before the rest of my teeth, and my weight has fluctuated by twenty pounds in one direction on the scale or the other since early adolescence. I've tried lifestyle changes, diets, periods of excessive exercise, fasting routines, and athletic commitments, but I still have days when I look in the mirror and feel unimpressed with my body.

I used to feel most content with my appearance when I was a hundred pounds. Now, whenever I see pictures of myself at that "ideal weight," I am genuinely shocked that I hadn't recognized how unhealthy I was at the time. Thankfully, I have grown out of that destructive desire to maintain such a low body weight. I've learned to feel best about my health when I'm exercising daily, minding what I'm eating, indulging from time to time, and listening to my body. Whether I'm in a great relationship with my body or treating it terribly, I try to focus on one goal: healthy not skinny.

I don't recall being explicitly told that skinny is better, and I wasn't bullied for being any particular size as a child. I think the pressure to be thin was a result of perceived societal expectations. I love walking through Target now and seeing ads with women of all different sizes, ages, and races, but most input from our culture at the macro-level communicates a different message. Many of the celebrities I admire are toned and thin. Ignoring all the work they put into maintaining their appearances—the personal trainers, dietitians, make up artists—I allow myself to be convinced that I need to be skinny in order to have value.

Healthy body image begins with beliefs. What are the messages that you receive from the world around you? What were you taught to expect of yourself and others? I am convinced I will struggle to accept my own skin and frame until I receive God's perspective of my value that He gave me. Don't be a slave to your beliefs. Submit them to the lordship of Christ. As our beliefs come into alignment with truth, our body images fall, slowly but surely, into alignment with health. We renounce expectations for ourselves that are not from God and begin to pursue physical health. We want to honor the temples He's given us to dwell in, not meet a certain standard of appearance.

Since I have started approaching health from a place of freedom and not striving, I don't feel controlled. I feel self-controlled. Body insecurity is no longer forcing me to go to the gym. I'm not giving up food I need or enjoy eating. I'm choosing to care for my body well as an act of praise to my Creator and an act of war against unfair societal expectations. Occasionally I fear that I'll always have to fight cravings or that I'll become less healthy as I age, but then I remember that there is no future for me without God. He will lead me then like He's leading me now. And I can't say what we will look like in heaven with glorified bodies, but from the sound of it, I don't think it will be too bad.

Sex

The Bible mentions sex many times, particularly sexual immorality. Sexual immorality may sound ominous, but it simply refers to ways we can dishonor God when it comes to sex. This doesn't mean there aren't ways we can honor God in sex, but the Bible tends to focus on the former. Relevant words we see throughout Scripture in reference to sexual immorality are fornication (sex outside of marriage), adultery (sex outside of marriage), and lust (sexual desire for someone outside of marriage).

Rape is clearly dishonoring to God. Consummating your marriage or conceiving a child with your spouse is honoring to God. Since the beginning, God established that sexual activity is meant to take place within a covenant between a husband and wife. He has given us sex as a gift, and how we use it matters. The problem I've seen is that people don't like talking about sexual immorality, and most who use their voices come across as offensive or judgmental in their passion for righteousness. Our goal is to avoid both those realities.

The general rule of thumb I like to abide by is from Paul in Ephesians 5:3, "But among you there must not be even a hint of sexual immorality, or of any kind of impurity, or of greed, because these are improper for God's holy people."

People get intense here because our salvation is at stake. Paul said, "Or do you not know that wrongdoers will not inherit the kingdom of God? Do not be deceived: neither the sexually immoral nor idolaters...will inherit the kingdom of God" (1 Corinthians 6:9-10). But that's nothing new. We knew we needed to become the righteousness of God through Jesus to inherit the kingdom. Jesus is the Hope for us, the grace that empowers us. Sexual immorality, though dangerous and serious, is not something we have to fear because we are more than conquerors through Christ.

Jesus told us that if we even think a lustful thought, we have committed adultery in God's eyes (Matthew 5:28), so it's a safe guess that sexual immorality is not something we want to flirt with. We also know that Jesus did not come to condemn the world but to save the world (John 3:17). So we have to remember that Jesus is rooting for our victory over and salvation from sin as we have conversations about sex.

People love to talk about sex. They have questions, fears, and general curiosity. We shouldn't be afraid of sex or avoid conversations about it. I believe God has thoughts about the gift of sex and the ways we communicate about sex to people who want to learn. In much of my experience, the Church has fallen short of doing that well, even with the best intentions. So when it's appropriate, I talk to other Christian women about sex and sexuality. I dialogue with no particular agenda and share wisdom when I feel prompted by the Spirit. The majority of those conversations with girls are miraculous. I get to watch their understanding shift from shame to confidence.

I will rarely force a conversation about sex. Instead, I wait for it to come up naturally. This could happen from talking about a movie a girl has seen, a response she has as I'm checking in on her relationship with her boyfriend, or as I share my own testimony about that spring break trip to Redding. I'm careful to listen attentively if they want to share a story with me in which they struggle with something related to sex. I'm equally available to answer any questions to the best of my ability or point them toward reliable resources for more information. The longer we are able to stay in the conversation, the more comfortable they are. After the first conversation, having another comes more naturally. They are able to express what they thought was too dark to share and be met with compassion and hope. I get to help them restore their perceptions of purity, self-esteem, intimacy, and boundaries.

Sometimes I am the first person a girl has ever told about the sexual trauma she's endured. Sometimes I am the first person to ever tell a girl that her thoughts, experiences, and feelings matter when it comes to sex. I get to be the messenger of God in their lives to tell them they aren't meant to live in shame. Being a safe haven for girls to find confidence in truth and love is one of my favorite parts of discipling.

I've learned that scare tactics aren't effective long-term. I try to avoid them now no matter what I'm discussing. Sometimes in our passion for righteousness, we come on too strong and intense. God is slow to anger and rich in love. I want to be like that, especially when it comes to something as personal as sex. STI's, unplanned pregnancies, broken relationships, and chemical bonds don't disappear when I choose not to talk about them. They're still risks and still potential conversation points, but I don't want to lead a child of God into making decisions based out of fear. Some might argue it's wisdom, not fear, that drives such conversations. I would argue there are wiser ways to impart wisdom.

Abstinence is never the goal; it's neutral ground. The Holy Spirit revealed this to me when I was reading Ezekiel. The chapter was about wickedness and righteousness, wicked acts and righteous acts. The basic sentiment was that we are not just called to avoid wickedness but to act righteously. I've talked with girls who grew up in Christian families and spent their whole lives avoiding the wrong thing. They live under the pressure of avoiding the "wrong path" at all times. The goal is righteousness, not simply abstinence.

In communicating healthy sexuality, I don't want to add pressure. There's an epidemic of young Christian women who have complications in their sex lives because up until marriage they had conditioned themselves to reject any sexual pleasure, desire, or expressions. I don't believe that was ever God's best for them. The fear of committing wicked acts leads to solely short-term results. The pressure of abstinence leads to a misunderstanding of God and missing out on God's intentions. Our aim should be righteousness. Righteousness comes not from focusing on avoiding wickedness but from following God. God offers purity, holiness, intimacy, passion, joy, confidence, empowerment, and comfort continuously within and outside of sexual activity.

Healthy sexuality outside of marriage looks like knowing we are deeply known and loved by God. That He is enough. We all have sex drives, but we are not slaves to our sex drives. I think of it like fasting. When I fast from food, I can still acknowledge that food is a good thing. But I abstain from eating as an act of honoring God and receiving more power through the Spirit in my life. I still get hungry, but I use that hunger to remind me to pray. I can even be around people who are eating, though it may be difficult, and choose not to eat myself.

Before we get married, we fast from sex. We can acknowledge it is good but abstain in reverence for God. We can recognize our sex drives but use that as an opportunity to focus on God and deny ourselves. We can even be around people who make decisions in their sex lives that we don't make for ourselves and still stand confident in our own decisions.

In developing healthy sexuality before marriage, I focus on developing self-control and a sense of self-worth that's not dependent on a partner. I cultivate ways to express passion and build connection with someone outside of sexual activity. I have fun and am filled with joy in other ventures. I gain knowledge of purity beyond just sex and experience all the benefits of being pure in heart like seeing God or entering into His presence (Psalm 24; Matthew 5).

Healthy sexuality within marriage is a continuation of all we've learned with God before another person was there, but now in marriage we enjoy the the added benefit of having sex. In singleness, I develop self-control to not look at someone lustfully, and in marriage I'll have self-control to not lust after others. In singleness, I break off my dependence on someone else to meet my needs, and in marriage I'll be able to restrain myself from depending on sex to maintain the relationship. In singleness, I remove the expectation that someone else can define my worth, and in marriage I'll get to know my worth without waiting for my husband's advances to establish it. There's less pressure to perform sexually because I'm confident I can express passion and build intimacy in other ways, so sex just gets to be a meaningful experience.

All this is just a glimpse of what I think God intends for healthy sexuality. He's the Giver of every good and perfect gift. Purity isn't strictly abstinence or celibacy—those are just the fruits of purity. They might be aspects of your sexuality in periods or for the entirety of your life, but they aren't the focus. The focus is who God is and what He has for you. God isn't oblivious to the fact that we have sexual needs and desires. He created us and said "it is good." He's not an uncomfortable parent avoiding the conversation or throwing books our way in hopes someone else will teach us all we need to know. He has good things for your marriage and sex life. He has good things for you today, regardless of your marital status. There's just more to life than sex, and singleness seems to be the God-given perfect time to explore all of that.

Physical Boundaries

When I talk with girls about sex, accidents are often a part of the conversation. She didn't mean to let it go that far. She didn't want to but she didn't say anything. She had been drinking. She felt pressured. She thought he loved her. She thought she loved him. And so on. Then I'm face to face with a girl who has been carrying shame about that night for sometimes years. I hate that. The mistake is bad, and it's sad as well. But what I really hate is how hard it is for her to own up to the mistake under the burden of shame and hopelessness. Too often a girl loses her value for sex when she loses her virginity. She's done it once, so why not do it again? This is why talking about physical boundaries and not perpetuating shame is important.

If you know and love your physical boundaries, you are far less likely to cross them. If you try to determine your boundaries in a heated moment, they're probably going to push the limits you would have established as if you had the time to think them out, pray over them, and ask a trusted mentor if they are sufficient for your stage of life. Once we establish boundaries, we know when we are getting close to doing something we might regret. We know when we are teetering on the brink of something dishonoring to God and we become aware of the ways we dance with sexual immorality.

What if we trusted the Holy Spirit enough to give us boundaries that fall in pleasant places? What if we let wise mentors and trusted friends comment on the decisions we make and actually take their caring advice into consideration? What if we searched out Scripture to find out what limitations God has set through the words of the apostles, prophets, and teachers that He appointed?

Those are the most beneficial questions I've reflected on and asked my girls about in order to navigate setting and maintaining physical boundaries. Boundaries in all scenarios are great because they allow us to play freely within the space we are given and not have to worry about how far is too far or which decisions are dangerous. Communicating physical boundaries should be a mutually-beneficial experience between you and your partner because it creates an environment of trust and safety. If your partner cannot understand that, now would be a great time to take inventory of whether or not your relationship should continue. No one should ever feel coerced, pressured, or forced to engage in activities they don't want to participate in.

Grace is a huge blessing we can cling to when it comes to boundaries. When lines get crossed and shame starts to creep in, it's time for you to speak up. Mistakes can feel like a trap door into condemnation. I used to try hiding my mistakes from God and from close friends. I didn't want to talk about them or think about them. But I ended up finding a friend who I felt comfortable enough with to confess my mistakes to in college. I had been reading in Galatians about crucifying the flesh and it's sinful desires. I knew that putting my flesh to death would be exposing and painful—that's what crucifixions were—but then those things in me would be dead. So I was bold and told my friend about the things I carried shame over.

She didn't throw a stone, she didn't victim-shame, she didn't do any of that. She told me God has better for me. We talked about what God might want to give me in place of shame that day and in place of making that mistake in the future. It brought me freedom which led me to enjoy life more. Be that friend to people. Accountability has a bad reputation a lot of times, but within the context of relationships, it's one of the greatest supports we can have.

When you feel like you could get carried away past your boundaries, just stop. A good partner will respect your decision—anyone else doesn't deserve you. Talk about the limitations you feel like God is leading you to set for yourself and your relationship. Communication will expose so much, and you may feel God lead you to "crucify" a sinful habit or activity you have partaken in apart or together. It may even feel painful to let go of. But it will create a gap that can be filled with a stronger relationship. Honesty pays off in situations like these. You find out sooner if someone is a good fit for you when you're fully yourself and you let them be themselves.

Shame is a trickster. We are tempted to choose shame when we have sinned because we think we have to earn our place back with God or maybe because we are afraid that we can't come before Him when we have sinned. We diminish the work of the Cross when we allow shame to enter into our lives. Sin creates a divide between us and God. Shame does the same thing. God desires neither. He wants to be in communion with us. I've learned so much about grace through my battles with shame. When I make a mistake intentionally or unintentionally and immediately choose to run to God, I find freedom and truth. It becomes a foundation to keep my feet secure and a fortress to protect me from the temptation of sin later.

In Song of Solomon 2, the bride's beloved says, "Catch for us the foxes; the little foxes that ruin the vineyard." Foxes represent disruptive, destructive distractions that negatively impact our relationships with God and others. Our beloved instructs us to catch the foxes. This includes whatever is taking away from your relationship with God– unhealthy coping mechanisms, inappropriate relationships, negative thought patterns, and so on. I pray for the grace to catch the foxes in my life because it reminds me that God is the one who invites me to catch the foxes. He never pressures us to get rid of them on our own. He has empowered us by His Spirit to remove those small habits and desires that destroy our abundant life through His love.

If you are struggling with sexual sin and feel like you'll never overcome it, that you have to fight it with your own strength, and that you want to hide—rejoice in this truth: It is finished. Jesus has already overcome. You have victory over it. Victory over sin is not in question—it's your irrevocable inheritance. God gave you authority to catch and kill every fox in your garden when He sacrificed Jesus. Jesus took that sin and shame on the cross, and He took it for your freedom. Your invitation now is to begin living in that freedom. Maybe you'll start living in it instantly. Maybe you'll live in it a little more every day and transform from one degree of glory to the next by the renewing of your mind. But it's yours. You get to co-labor with God.

Set up accountability and boundaries. Ask God to give you strength, wisdom, and support. You were never going to beat this struggle in your own strength anyway, so let God do it for you. Just go along with Him. In every challenging moment, He is with you. In every mistake you make, He will rescue you. His grace is sufficient for you. Let Him hem you in behind and before, and lay His hand upon you. Ask Him where the boundaries are. You'll find they've fallen in pleasant places (Psalm 16).

Forgiveness

A friend described me as burning with care. I think it's a trait I inherited from my mother, and I love it. It comes out most intensely when it comes to social justice. I don't have the tolerance to watch movies or TV shows with rape and sex trafficking. It makes me sick and hugely angry, even in fictional shows, because I know those injustices happen to real people every single day. It's a tragedy. It's rare that I meet a girl who hasn't experienced some sort of unwanted advances from a man. Women have shared a wide range of sexual misconduct directed towards them, from inappropriate texts to non-consensual intercourse. The same could be said for men, but I don't engage in many conversations about sex with men.

Victim-shaming is not okay. I feel like I don't need to expound on that. I would, however, encourage you to re-read the chapter on empowerment if you feel stuck in a victim-mindset because of what someone has done to you. You didn't deserve that. So many people want to take responsibility for when they were sexually harassed or assaulted. They say things like "If I hadn't been drinking..." or "If I hadn't walked down that street...".

People will tell them "If you hadn't had worn that then..." or "You were asking for it when you..." That's not okay either. Walking is wisdom is your responsibility, yes. Upholding your boundaries is your responsibility, too. But no one is justified in infringing on your personal rights.

One of the most impactful moments with one of my past disciplers occurred after I heard Abi and Justin Stumvoll, founders of the Connected Life podcast, give a live talk about sex. The boldness with which they spoke about their freedom from sin and shame inspired me to be brave. I felt safe in the promise of freedom to share with my discipler about a situation involving sexual misconduct that had taken place in my inner circle. I unloaded all the shame and confusion I had been storing up because I felt like I couldn't talk to anyone about it. I definitely couldn't talk to the person involved about it, and I felt afraid but also angry around the person. My discipler responded by saying, "That's not okay you were put in that situation, and it's not your fault." I felt so free, so released from the mess.

God has placed people in our lives for us to love. They weren't put there so we could live in fear or for anger to divide us. We are more than conquerors. So from there, I began my process of forgiveness toward everyone involved in the situation.

Forgiveness is hard, especially when we have been hurt or wronged in a very deep way. But when I think of how God still chose to sacrifice His Son for us, despite how far we fell, I'm compelled to forgive. The difficulty of forgiveness pays off in full. The freedom it brings is worth the struggle to walk in it every time. I would challenge you to go through your sexual history in your mind, with a mentor, or with a counselor and begin releasing people who crossed your boundaries from your prison of unforgiveness.

From your first crush to your greatest heartbreak, where

have you been hurt and who can you forgive? You don't have to contact people, reconnect, or rebuild relationships. Between you and God, let go of the wrong that's been done to you and let God heal those places. You'll find yourself needing less validation from people you're attracted to, feeling less pressure to perform for who you're involved with, and living in more confidence and security with your physicality.

When I meet with girls who have been taken advantage of, a current of rage flows beneath my compassion for them. No one should be treated that way. It's hard to come to grips with when you hear the trauma that someone you love has endured. I have deep, sincere concern for those who have been treated this way. I'm sorry. I hope that God will speak into your pain and bring you peace.

God asks us to forgive. It's important to Him. He is entirely just and still requires forgiveness from us. The two aren't meant to conflict with one another. God is our very source of forgiveness; He set the standard at the Cross. God offered us forgiveness first through the blood of His son. Forgiveness toward your abuser may sound impossible, but you don't have to do it through your own strength and will. The Holy Spirit can get you there.

If forgiveness wasn't the best thing for you, He wouldn't ask it of you. So I encourage those of you who have experienced trauma to begin that conversation with God when you're ready. Be honest and tell Him if it makes you angry, scared, heartbroken. The process may ignite feelings of betrayal or mistrust toward God. Allow Him to respond to the emotions that arise. He has things to say about what you endured. He'll heal those places in your heart because He's good. It's His promise to you to make all the wrong things right.

God's forgiveness is so much greater than we can comprehend. He offered forgiveness motivated by love to the worst criminals, dictators, and tyrants the world has seen. His love isn't given or withheld based on the degree to which we sinned against him. We can live in the freedom of that kind of forgiveness by His grace. We don't need to hide behind personal rights; we need to walk in forgiveness—to live in the death, resurrection, and ascension of Christ. We can establish boundaries with the grace to turn the other cheek if we've been sinned against.

If you were wronged, Jesus may be the greatest Friend to

relate to you. He set the example of crying out to the Father and letting the Holy Spirit revive Him when He was wronged. Jesus said on the cross, "Father, forgive them because they don't understand what they're doing." He was in His greatest moment of pain and still looked to the Father for their forgiveness. Afterwards, the Spirit of God resurrected Him in the greatest miracle the world has ever witnessed. Jesus then ascended to sit at the right hand of the Father. Now He reigns for all eternity in perfect healing and wholeness, and invites us to do the same. That victory is available to you through grace if you are willing to forgive as well. Jesus doesn't ask us lightly to forgive. He communicates with intense compassion that forgiveness is an essential kingdom value (Matthew 6:15).

For me, I would rather fail and persevere as I become like Christ than harden my heart and pridefully wait for a miraculous work of God to redeem the situation. So I take steps toward forgiveness for the people who have wronged me, for the people who have wronged my loved ones, and to the people I see on the news when I can't understand how much evil can exist in this world. God sees it too. Our faithfulness to what He has asked of us is all that we are responsible for. He'll take care of the rest. He takes care of His own.

You have also probably wronged someone. Sometimes we explain our behaviors away or bury them deep in silence and shame. If you can repent and ask for forgiveness from that person, absolutely do that. If you are no longer able to speak with that person, talk to God about the ways you sinned against them. Release yourself from the mistakes you've made. Love will cover you in them; grace will teach you from them. We have all been victims and perpetrators to some degree. Neither of those are our identities. We have been called by new names and adopted into a royal family. Our sins were forgiven the moment we put our trust in God, so now we just get to live like it. The truth sets us free, and we are free indeed.

Love

We know we are becoming miracles to the world when we look like love because God is love. Praise God that His love is not restricted and our transformation into His likeness is not limited. Love is flowing through us, making us brave, carrying us through the day, keeping us pure, making us holy, and reminding us of hope. Love is so unfathomably great that I feel both humbled and sustained in my exploration of it.

Finding a working definition of love is quite the task. In college, we learned about Sternberg's Triangular Theory of Love, which explored the combinations of essential aspects of love: intimacy, commitment, and passion. But this explanation of love lacks a concrete definition. Maslow's Hierarchy of Needs presents love as one of the primary needs of an individual, including family, friendship, intimacy, connection, and belonging as aspects of love's nature. But, this too, does not encompass all of the aspects of love. The Bible talks about what love is like: patient, kind, not envious, not boastful, not proud, not self-seeking, and so on. Still, we don't know what it is. I've heard opinions on love: it's a feeling, it's a choice, it's madness, it's blindness, it's chemical, it's physical, it's emotional, it's spiritual. It's adoration, attraction, attachment. Love can be sacrificial and unconditional or it can be miscarried and impulsive. It can be nurturing and compassionate or arousing and burning.

Abrahamic religions believe we were created because of God's love, and thus, we live to return love to Him and each other. Indian religions like Buddhism, Sikhism, and Hinduism believe that love is necessary for enlightenment, sacramental, and highly virtuous. All of these dogmas of love piece together a universal longing for this beautiful enigma.

I don't have an infallible definition myself. I know that God is love. Love grounds us in truth and also frees us from fear. It can extend from the heart, soul, mind, and body. It can bind together lovers, enemies, and all in between. Love is stronger than anything and is the sole satisfaction for human nature's deepest desire. I am convinced that the world craves love. I sense it in the conversations I have with people. I see the desperation for it in glimpses of the world from romantic comedies to action films, from dating scripts to human trafficking. I recognize it in myself from how desperately I want to be wanted.

I would argue all of our efforts are in pursuit of love. Love of God, love of others, love of self all motivate us to live, to engage, and to choose. When reflecting on our decisions, we can trace them back to whether we felt the presence or absence of love. For example, people usually choose to make love out of an overflow of mutual love for another or an attempt to attain unrequited love.

We will feel extraordinarily more confident in ourselves when we acknowledge our need for love and our unending access to it in Christ. He created us for love. Our longing for love can lead us to many people, places, or things, but it should always lead us back to Him. In celibacy or abstinence, we were never intended for lack. We are invited to know love's width, length, depth, and height. No matter who you are and what your history is, you can be satisfied in God. At the very least, you can be content in your pursuit of finding Love.

Above all, love. We have nothing apart from it. We all want it. Be love both to people who know it well and others who have rarely seen it. Receive it and give it away extravagantly. Choose it over and over. When all is said and done, let there be love. This entire book could be viewed as a new list of rules—do's and don'ts for how to live. You could try to write out all my advice and try and implement it, but you would fail. I would fail.

Jesus says, "I am the vine; you are the branches. If you remain in me and I in you, you will bear much fruit. Apart from me you can do nothing." (John 15:5) Our best bet is to receive the love of God and allow Him to transform our lives—that's how good fruit begins to grow.

My best definition of love is this: love is a miracle. It is surprising, divine, inexplicable, and God-given. Love is the power to redeem the world one miracle at a time. It sustains your very life and drives you in your purpose.

You have love in you that will never run dry and can never be broken. Most importantly, you have always been and will ever be loved. Love never fails.

Death can't kill it, life can't not break it, spirits can't steal it —nothing in existence can overcome it. Today could not take it away anymore than tomorrow could shatter it. In the blueprints of His creation, God made certain that nothing would ever be powerful enough to separate you from His love. Love is yours, always and forever. You will be loved for all of eternity.

To My Girls,

All of you, who I have discipled and who I have yet to meet, thank you for reading this book. I'm excited that you've reached the end, and hope you feel excited to go live your life well. I've been praying that the Holy Spirit would be with you and gracefully lead you into more freedom as you read. I believe in you and the ability you have to bring truth and love into the world. I dream of standing in the wake of your influence as you impact the world empowered by God. But even if I never get to see the wonders your life produces, I know you are the miracle that can reveal the grace and power of God to your world.

For you and me, God is all. Protect that relationship, honor it, cherish it. God will always be faithful to you. Life will be wild, but God will be constant—or maybe it's the other way around. God's love is an endless adventure; life is just life. Don't put too much pressure on yourself to figure everything out; just give into Love.

Show yourself the same love and respect that God has for you. You aren't a slave to fear anymore or ever will be again. You're His child. Give yourself a chance to be loved and to belong. Give yourself the space to be brave. As Jesus sits at the right hand of the Father now, He's thinking of you. You're not a second thought. You're not a burden or extra responsibility. You're the desire of His heart. He wants you.

You know what thread binds together the heroes of our faith? Faith. Abraham, Moses, Paul, Peter, you and me—we all have a conviction of what is not yet seen that has and will transform the world around us. Live by that faith and not by what you see. People can be changed by knowing the Spirit of God in you. It doesn't take brilliant strategy or perfect execution, just obedience to God who loves the world. So have fun. It's a joyful life to show people sparks of light in the darkness they know.

My prayer for you now is that God will bring you good people, wise counsel, and supportive friends that you will be courageous enough to open up to. I pray you always find someone to pour into you and someone you can pour into—that your life will be a rushing river, not stagnant. And I pray the testimony of Jesus in your life will piece together the testimonies of Jesus in the lives around you.

Love,

    Savannah

P.S. I would love to connect with you to talk about what God is doing in your life and ministry. You can get in touch with me at savannahugan@gmail.com.

Notes

Adichie, Chimamanda Ngozi. We Should All Be Feminists. New York, Anchor Books, 2015, pp. 27-29.

Nichols, Wallace J. Blue Mind. 1st ed., New York, Little, Brown and Company, July 2014.

Tozer, A.W. The Knowledge of the Holy. 1st ed., New York, HarperCollins Publishers, 1961, p. 1.

Made in the USA
Columbia, SC
12 July 2020